The Early Journal of Charles Wesley

Beginnings of a Great Christian Hymnist

By Charles Wesley

PANTIANOS
CLASSICS

Published by Pantianos Classics

ISBN-13: 978-1-78987-652-9

First published in 1909

Contents

Prefatory Note

The manuscript Journal of Charles Wesley was purchased from his son and namesake, and is now preserved at the Methodist Publishing House. It is bound in parchment, measures 7¾ x 5 inches, and is two inches thick. Thomas Jackson tells us that it had been found among some loose straw on the floor of a warehouse where the furniture of Charles Wesley, Junior, was deposited. He purchased it and other manuscripts in 1829, on behalf of the Conference, used it in writing his *Life of Charles Wesley* in 1841, and prepared it for the press in 1849. It begins with Charles Wesley's arrival at Frederica, a month after the brothers 'first set foot on American ground,' and closes on November 6, 1756. There are some gaps in the record which a student of Early Methodism deeply regrets, but the Journal is only surpassed by that of his brother as a picture of the difficulties in Georgia, the happy scenes of Whit Week 1738, and the first days of the Evangelical Revival, with the triumphs of the field preaching, the perils of the mob, and the gradual spread of Methodism over England.

In this volume the story is carried down to August 27, 1739, and two more volumes would complete the Journal. It is hoped that the sale will justify their publication, for they show that the Poet of Methodism was as zealous and untiring an evangelist as his brother, and give welcome glimpses of the way in which some of his hymns were born amid the exciting scenes of his itinerancy.

The Rev. Nehemiah Curnock has with great patience and skill deciphered some of the short hand passages of the Journal, which bring out more clearly the conditions under which the poet's life in Georgia was spent. These passages are placed between square brackets. To Mr. Curnock all students of Wesley's life are deeply indebted, and the extensive notes in his new edition of *John Wesley's Journal* throw light on many passages in his brother's record.

Names are given as Charles Wesley wrote them, but blanks have been filled in where fresh information has made this possible.

The following dates from the writer's *Life of Charles Wesley* may be useful for reference.

1707. Charles Wesley born December 18.
1716. Entered Westminster School.
1726. Elected to Christ Church, Oxford.
1735. October 14, embarked for Georgia.

1736. February 6, lands at Savannah.
     July 26, starts for England.
     December 2, arrives at Deal.
1738. May 21, evangelical conversion.
     July, helps Mr. Stonehouse at Islington.
1739. May 29, becomes a field preacher.
     Hymns and Sacred Poems published.
1749. April 8, marriage to Sarah Gwynne.
1788. March 29, died in Marylebone.

JOHN TELFORD.

December, 1909.

The Journal of the Rev. Charles Wesley, M.A.

1736

Tuesday, *March* 9. About three in the afternoon, I first set foot on St. Simon's island, and immediately my spirit revived. No sooner did I enter upon my ministry than God gave me, like Saul, another heart. So true is that [remark] of Bishop Hall: 'The calling of God never leaves a man unchanged; neither did God ever employ any one in His service whom He did not enable to the work He set him; especially those whom He raises up to the supply of His place, and the representation of Himself.' The people, with Mr. Oglethorpe, were all arrived the day before.

The first who saluted me on my landing was honest Mr. Ingham, and that with his usual heartiness. Never did I more rejoice at the sight of him; especially when he told me the treatment he has met with for vindicating the Lord's day: such as every minister of Christ must meet with. The people seemed overjoyed to see me; Mr. Oglethorpe in particular received me very kindly.

I spent the afternoon in conference with my parishioners. (With what trembling ought I to call them mine!) At seven we had evening prayers, in the open air, at which Mr. Oglethorpe was present. The lesson gave me the fullest direction and greatest encouragement: 'Continue instant in prayer, and watch in the same with thanksgiving; withal praying also for us, that God would open unto us a door of utterance, to speak the mystery of Christ; that I may make it manifest, as I ought to speak. Walk in wisdom toward them that are without, redeeming the time. Let your speech be alway with grace, seasoned with salt, that ye may know how ye ought to answer every man.' 'Say to Archippus, Take heed to the ministry which thou hast received of the Lord, that thou fulfil it.' (Col. iv. 2-6, 17.) At nine I returned, and lay in the boat.

Wednesday, March 10. Between five and six in the morning I read short prayers to a few at the fire, before Mr. Oglethorpe's tent, in a hard shower of rain. Mr. Oglethorpe had set up a tent for the women, near his own. Toward noon I found an opportunity of talking at the tent-door with Mrs. Welch. I laboured to guard her against the cares of the world and to give herself to God in the Christian sacrifice; but to no purpose. God was pleased not to add weight to my words; therefore they could make no impression.

After dinner I began talking with Mrs. Germain, about baptizing her child by immersion. She was much averse to it, though she owned it a strong, healthy child. I then spoke to her husband, who was soon satisfied, and brought his wife to be so too.

In the evening I endeavoured to reconcile Mrs. Welch to Mrs. Hawkins, (Note: These women embittered the life of the Wesleys in Georgia. See Standard edition John Wesley's *Journal*, Vol. I. pp. 188-9.) who, I assured her, bore her no ill-will. She replied, You must not tell me that. Mrs. Hawkins is a very subtle woman. I understand her perfectly. There is a great man in the case, therefore I cannot speak; only that she is exceedingly jealous of me. Company stopped her saying more.

Thursday, March 11. At ten this morning I began the full service, to about a dozen women whom I had got together; intending to continue it, and only to read a few prayers to the men before they went to work. I also expounded the second lesson with some boldness, as I had a few times before.

After prayers I met Mrs. Hawkins's maid, in a great passion of tears, at being struck by her mistress. She seemed resolved to make away with her self, to escape her Egyptian bondage. With much difficulty I prevailed upon her to return, and carried her back to her mistress. Upon my asking Mrs. Hawkins to forgive her she refused me with the utmost roughness, rage, and almost reviling.

Mr. Tackner, whom I talked with next, made me full amends. He was in an excellent temper; resolved to strive, not with his wife, but himself, in putting off the old man, and putting on the new.

In the evening I heard the first harsh word from Mr. Oglethorpe, when I asked for something for a poor woman. The next day I was surprised by a rougher answer in a matter that deserved still greater encouragement. I knew not how to account for his increasing coldness.

My encouragement was the same in speaking with Mrs. Welch, whom I found all storm and tempest. The meek, the teachable Mrs. Welch (that *was* in the ship) was now so wilful, so untractable, so fierce, that I could not bear to stay near her. I did not mend myself by stumbling again upon Mr. Oglethorpe, who was with the men under arms, in expectation of an enemy. I stayed as long as I could, however,

> Unsafe within the wind
> Of such commotion:

but at last the hurricane of his passion drove me away.

Sunday, March 14. We had prayers under a great tree. In the Epistle I was plainly shown what I ought to be, and what to expect. 'Giving no offence in anything, that the ministry be not blamed: but in all things approving ourselves as the ministers of God, in much patience, in afflictions, in necessities, in distresses, in stripes, in imprisonments, in tumults, in labours, in watchings, in fastings; by pureness, by knowledge, by longsuffering, by kindness, by the Holy Ghost, by love unfeigned, by the word of truth, by the power of God, by the armour of righteousness on the right hand and on the left, by honour and dishonour, by evil report and good report: as deceivers, and yet true; as unknown, and yet well known; as dying, and, behold, we live; as chastened, and not killed; as sorrowful, yet alway rejoicing; as poor, yet making many rich; as having nothing, and yet possessing all things.' (2 Cor. vi. 3-10.)

I preached with boldness, on singleness of intention, to about twenty people, among whom was Mr. Oglethorpe. Soon after, as he was in Mrs. Hawkins's hut, a bullet (through the carelessness of one of the people who were exercising to-day) flew through the wall, close by him.

Mrs. Germain now retracted her consent for having her child baptized; however, Mrs. Colwell's I did baptize by trine immersion, before a numerous congregation.

At night I found myself exceeding faint, but had no better bed to go to than the ground; on which I slept very comfortably, before a great fire, and waked the next morning perfectly well.

Tuesday, March 16. I was wholly spent in writing letters for Mr. Oglethorpe. I would not spend six days more in the same manner for all Georgia.

Wednesday, March 17. I found an opportunity to tell Mrs. Welch the reason why I had not talked with her lately was my despair of doing her any good. She acknowledged herself entirely changed, but could never tell me the cause. I immediately guessed it, and mentioned my conjecture. She confessed the truth of it. My soul was filled with pity; and I prayed God the sin of others might not ruin her.

Thursday, March 18. To-day Mr. Oglethorpe set out with the Indians, to hunt the buffalo upon the main, and to see the utmost limits of what they claimed. In the afternoon Mrs. Welch discovered to me the whole mystery of iniquity.

[The record of her vile accusations is in short hand and closes with the words, 'With a brief prayer I instructed her to trust in God and persuaded her to seek for satisfaction only in the means of grace. That ended her.']

Went to my myrtle-walk, where, as I was repeating 'I will thank Thee, for Thou hast heard me, and art become my salvation,' a gun was fired from the other side of the bushes. Providence had that moment turned me from that end of the walk which the shot flew through; but I heard them pass close by me.

Sunday, March 21. Mr. Oglethorpe had ordered, oftener than once, that no man should shoot on a Sunday. Germain had been committed to the guard-room for it in the morning, but was, upon his submission, released. In the midst of the sermon a gun was fired. Davison, the constable, ran out, and found it was the Doctor; told him it was contrary to orders, and he was obliged to desire him to come to the officer. Upon this the Doctor flew into a great passion, and said, 'What, do not you know I am not to be looked upon as a common fellow?' Not knowing what to do, the constable went, and returned, after consulting with Hermsdorf, with two sentinels, and brought him to the guard-room. Hereupon Mrs. Hawkins charged and fired a gun; and then ran thither, like a madwoman, crying she had shot, and would be confined too. The constable and Hermsdorf persuaded her to go away. She cursed and swore in the utmost transport of passion, threatening to kill the first man that should come near her. Alas, my brother! what has become of thy hopeful convert?

In the afternoon, while I was talking in the street with poor Catherine, her mistress came up to us, and fell upon me with the utmost bitterness and scurrility; said she would blow me up, and my brother, whom she once thought honest, but was now undeceived; that I was the cause of her husband's confinement; but she would be revenged, and expose my d__d hypocrisy, my prayers four times a day by beat of drum, and abundance more, which I cannot write, and thought no woman, though taken from Drury Lane, could have spoken. I only said I pitied her, but defied all she or the devil could do; for she could not hurt me. I was strangely preserved from passion, and at parting told her I hoped she would soon come to a better mind.

In the evening hour of retirement I resigned myself to God, in my brother's prayer for conformity to a suffering Saviour.

I was interrupted by the following note.

['MR. WESLEY,

['Being by your priestly order confined, the care of the sick is no longer incumbent on me. As you have been busy in intermeddling with my affairs, I request, sir, the following patients may have proper assistance, which hitherto has been before this time, and no neglect laid to your injured friend John Hawkins.

['PS. I dispute they have right of confining a surgeon, and especially for a day in confinement.'

[After a short prayer for meekness I went and visited all his patients, only saying, 'I had no hand in your confinement. The gun was fired in sermon time, and before the constable came back I went directly in my surplice to the tent and gave the sacrament. Immediately after this I took a walk in the woods, whence I did not return till dinner time, about an hour after your confinement, which I then first heard of. You may understand __ __ if you say he ascribes it to me. He wholly denies it.'

['And when you did confess it, he replied, why did you not tell him he had no business or liberty to confine me, no more than a captain his lieutenant?'

['Because I did presume they understood their own business best; and your having charged the matter upon me made me resolve to have no concern in it.' Going from home I was informed of the compliments Mrs. Hawkins was very surely paying my brother and me.

[*Monday, March* 22. While I was persuading Mr. Welch not to concern himself in this disturbance, I heard Mrs. Hawkins cry out 'Murder!' and walked away. Returning out of the woods, I was informed by Mr. Welch that poor blockhead Mrs. Welch had joined with Mrs. Hawkins and the devil in their slanders of me. I would not believe it till half the town told me the same, and exclaimed against her ingratitude. Soon after Haydon informed me that he had civilly told Mrs. Hawkins his orders were not to suffer her to come within the camp, but he would carry those bottles for her. She replied she would come, and, upon his holding open his arms to hinder her, broke one of the bottles on his head. He caught her in his arms, she striking him continually and crying out 'Murder!' Hawkins at the same time ran up and struck him. He closed and threw him down, set his foot upon him, and said if he resisted he would run his bayonet into him. Mark Hird, the other constable, was meantime engaged in keeping off Mrs. Hawkins, who broke the other bottle on his head. Welch coming up to her assistance, Davison the constable desired him to keep off the camp. Nevertheless he ran upon him, took the gun out of his hand, and struck him with all his might on his sides and face; till Haydon interposed and parted them. Welch then ran and gave the Doctor a bayonet, which was immediately taken from him. Mrs. Hawkins cried out continually against the parsons, and swore revenge against my brother and me. But the bridle is in her mouth.

[At three I carried Mrs. Perkins to Mrs. Welch; but finding her as the troubled sea, thought this no time for expostulating with her treatment of me. Asked whether I could do anything for her or her husband, now confined for his violence towards the officers, her railing forced me to leave her.

[Mr. Hird soon after told me he had followed Mrs. Hawkins to her house, and entreated her to return quietly to her husband and trouble the common peace no longer. Upon no greater provocation than this, she snatched up an iron pistol and offered to strike him. She presented it, but was seized before she could discharge it. The pistol, gun, and other arms were now taken from her, and she put in a guard of two sentinels.]

Faint and weary with the day's fatigue, I found my want of true holiness, and begged God to give me comfort from His Word. I then read, in the evening lesson, 'But thou, O man of God, flee these things; and follow after righteousness, godliness, faith, love, patience, meekness. Fight the good fight of faith, lay hold on eternal life, whereunto thou art called, and hast professed a good profession before many witnesses.' (1 Tim. vi. 11, 12.) Before prayers I took a walk with Mr. Ingham, who was surprised I should not think innocence a sufficient protection. I had not indeed acquainted him with what Mrs. Welch had told me. At night I was forced to exchange my usual bed, the ground, for a chest, being almost speechless through a violent cold.

Tuesday, March 23. In reading Heb. xi., I felt my faith revive; and I was confident God would either turn aside the trial, or strengthen me to bear it. In the afternoon Mr. Davison informed me the Doctor had sent his wife word to arm herself from the case of instruments, and forcibly make her escape; to speak to Mr. Oglethorpe first, and even to stab any that should oppose her. Mrs. Perkins told me she had heard Mrs. Hawkins say 'Mr. Oglethorpe dares not punish me.' I was encouraged by the lesson: 'God hath not given us the spirit of fear; but of power, and of love, and of a sound mind. Be not thou therefore ashamed of the testimony of our Lord, nor of me His prisoner: but be thou partaker of the afflictions of the gospel according to the power of

God.' 'Whereunto I am appointed a preacher. For the which cause I also suffer these things: nevertheless I am not ashamed: for I know whom I have believed, and am persuaded that He is able to keep that which I have committed unto Him against that day.' (2 Tim. i. 7, 8, 11, 12.)

Wednesday, March 24. I was enabled to pray earnestly for my enemies, particularly Mr. Oglethorpe, whom I now looked upon as the chief of them. Then I gave myself up entirely to God's disposal, desiring I might not now want power to pray, when I most of all needed it. Mr. Ingham then came, and read the thirty-seventh Psalm: a glorious exhortation to patience, and confidence in God, from the different estate of the good and wicked. After breakfast I again betook myself to intercession, particularly for Mrs. Welch, that Satan, in the shape of that other bad woman, might not stand at her right hand. Doubting whether I should not interpose for the prisoners, I consulted the oracle, and met Jer. xliv. 16, 17: 'As for the word which thou hast spoken to us in the name of the Lord, we will not hearken unto it: but we will certainly do whatsoever thing goeth forth out of our own mouth.' This determined me not to meddle with them at all.

At eleven I met Mrs. Perkins, who told me of the infamy Mrs. Hawkins has brought on Mr. Oglethorpe, and the utter discouragement it will be to the people if she is supported. Farther she informed me that Mrs. Welch begins to repent of having engaged so far with her, confessing she has done it through cowardice, as thinking Mr. Oglethorpe will bear her out against all the world.

Soon after I talked with Mrs. Welch, and with the last degree of astonishment heard her accuse herself. Horror of horrors! Never did I feel such excess of pity. I gave myself up to prayer for her. Mr. Ingham soon joined me. All the prayers expressed a full confidence in God: when notice was given us of Mr. Oglethorpe's landing. Mrs. Hawkins, Mr. Ingham, and myself were sent for. We found him in his tent with the people round it; Mr. and Mrs. Hawkins within. After a short hearing, the officers were reprimanded, and the prisoners dismissed. At going out Mrs. Hawkins modestly told me she had something more to say against me, but would take another time. I only answered, 'You know, madam, it is impossible for *me* to fear *you*.' When they were gone, Mr. Oglethorpe said he was convinced and glad I had had no hand in all this. I told him I had something to impart, of the last importance, when he was at leisure. He took no notice, but read his letters; and I walked away with Mr. Ingham, who was utterly astonished. The issue is just what I expected.

I was struck with those words in the evening lesson: Thou therefore, my son, be strong in the grace that is in Christ Jesus. Endure hardness, as a good soldier of Jesus Christ. Remember that Jesus Christ was raised from the dead, according to my gospel: wherein I suffer trouble, as an evil-doer, even unto bonds; but the word of God is not bound. Therefore I endure all things for the elect's sakes, that they may also obtain the salvation which is in Christ Jesus with eternal glory. It is a faithful saying: For if we be dead with Him, we shall also live with Him: if we suffer, we shall also reign with Him. (2 Tim. ii. 1, 3, 8-12.) After reading I could not forbear adding, 'I need say nothing. God will shortly apply this.'

Glory be to God for my confidence hitherto! Oh, what am I if left to myself? but I can do and suffer all things through Christ strengthening me.

Thursday, March 25. At five I heard the second drum beat for prayers, which I had desired Mr. Ingham to read, being much weakened by my fever. But considering I ought to appear at this time especially, I rose and heard those animating words: 'If any man serve Me, let him follow Me; and where I am, there shall also My servant be: if any man serve Me, him will My Father honour. Now is My soul troubled; and what shall I say? Father, save Me from this hour: but for this cause came I unto this hour. Father, glorify Thy name.' (John xii. 26-8.)

At half-hour past seven Mr. Oglethorpe called me out of my hut. I looked up to God, and went. He charged me with mutiny and sedition; with stirring up the people to desert the colony. Accordingly he said they had had a meeting last night, and sent a message to him this morning, desiring leave to go; that their speaker had informed against them, and me the spring of all; that the men were such as constantly came to prayers, therefore I must have instigated them; that he should not scruple shooting half a dozen of them at once; but that he had, out of kindness, *first* spoke to me. My answer was: 'I desire, sir, you would have no regard to my brothers, my friends, or the love you had for me, if anything of this is made out against me. I know nothing of their meeting or designs. Of those you have mentioned, not one comes constantly to prayers, or sacrament. I never incited any one to leave the colony. I desire to answer my accuser face to face.' He told me my accuser was Mr. Lawley, whom he would bring if I would wait here. I added, 'Mr. Lawley is a man who has declared he knows no reason for keeping fair with any man, but a design to get all he can by him: but there was nothing to be got by the poor parsons.' I asked whether he himself was not assured that there were enough men in Frederica to say or swear anything against any man that should be in disgrace: whether, if he himself was removed, or succeeded ill, the whole stream of the people would not be turned against him; and even this Lawley, who was of all others the most violent in condemning the prisoners and justifying the officers. I observed this was the old cry, 'Away with the Christians to the lions'; mentioned H. and his wife's scandalizing my brother and me, and vowing revenge against us both, threatening me yesterday even in his presence. I asked what redress or satisfaction was due to my character; what good I could do in my present parish if cut off by their calumnies from ever seeing one half of it. I ended with assuring him I had and should still make it my business to promote peace among all. I felt no disturbance while speaking, but lifted up my heart to God, and found Him present with me. While Mr. Oglethorpe was fetching Lawley I thought of our Lord's words: 'Ye shall be brought before governors and kings for My sake. But when they deliver you up, take no thought how or what ye shall speak: for it shall be given you in that same hour what ye shall speak' (Matt. x. 18, 19); and applied to Him for help, and words to make my defence.

Before Mr. Oglethorpe returned I called in upon Mr. Ingham, and desired him to pray for me; then walked, and, musing on the event, opened the book on Acts xv. 31-3: 'Which when they had read, they rejoiced for the consolation; and...exhorted the brethren with many words, and confirmed them. And after they had tarried there a space, they were let go in peace.' Mr. Ingham coming, I related all that had passed. On sight of Mr. Oglethorpe and Lawley, he retired.

Mr. Oglethorpe observed the place was too public. I offered to carry him to my usual walk in the woods. On our way God put it into my heart to say, 'Show only the least disinclination to find me guilty, and you shall see what a turn it will give to the accusation.' He took the hint, and instead of calling upon Lawley to make good his charge, began with the quarrel in general; but did not show himself angry with me, or desirous to find me to blame. Lawley, who appeared full of guilt and fear, upon this dropped his accusation, or shrunk it into my 'forcing the people to prayers.' I replied, that the people themselves would acquit me of that; and as to the officers' quarrel, I appealed to the officers for the truth of my assertion, that I had had no hand at all in it; professed my desire and resolution of promoting peace and obedience: and as to the people, I was persuaded their desire of leaving the colony arose from mistake, not malice. Here Mr. Oglethorpe spoke of reconciling matters; bade Lawley tell the petitioners he would not so much as ask who they were, if they were but quiet for the future. 'I hope,' added he, 'they will be so; and Mr. Wesley here hopes so too.' 'Yes, sir,' says Lawley, 'I really believe it of Mr. Wesley, and had always a very great respect for him.' I turned, and said to Mr. Oglethorpe, 'Did not I tell you it would be so?' He replied to Lawley, 'Yes; you had always a very great respect for Mr. Wesley. You told me he was a stirrer-up of sedition, and at the bottom of all this disturbance.' With this gentle reproof he dismissed him; and I thanked him for having first spoken to me of what I was accused of, begging he would always do so. This he promised, and then I walked with him to Mrs. Hawkins's door. She came out aghast to see me with him. He there left me, 'and I was delivered out of the mouth of the lion.'

I went to my hut, where I found Mr. Ingham. He told me this was but the beginning of sorrows. 'Not as I will, but as Thou wilt.' About noon, in the midst of a violent storm of thunder and lightning, I read the eighteenth Psalm, and found it gloriously suited to my circumstances. I never felt the Scriptures as now. Now I need them I find them all written for my instruction and comfort. At the same time I feel great joy in the expectation of our Saviour thus coming to judgement, when the secrets of all hearts shall be revealed, and God shall make my innocency as clear as the light, and my just dealing as the noonday.

At three I walked with Mr. Ingham, and read him the history of this amazing day. We rejoiced together in the protection of God, and through comfort of the Scriptures.

The evening lesson was full of encouragement. 'This know also, that in the last days perilous times shall come. For men shall be...*false accusers,* incontinent, fierce, despisers of those that are good, traitors, heady, high-minded, *...But they shall proceed no further:* for their folly shall be made manifest unto all men. But thou hast fully known my doctrine, manner of life, ...what persecutions I endured; but out of them all the Lord delivered me. Yea, and all that will live godly in Christ Jesus shall suffer persecution. But evil men and seducers shall wax worse and worse, deceiving, and being deceived...All Scripture is given by inspiration of God, and is profit able for doctrine, for reproof, for correction, for instruction in righteousness.' (2 Tim. iii. 1-4, 9-13, 16.) Blessed be God, I begin to find it so!

Meeting with Mr. Hird, I persuaded him to use all his interest with the people to lay aside all thoughts of leaving the colony. He told me he had assured Mr. Oglethorpe that this was always my language toward him and the rest; but was answered short with, 'You must not tell me that; I know better.'

After spending an hour at the camp in singing such Psalms as suited the occasion, I went to bed in the hut, which was thoroughly wet with the day's rain.

Friday, March 26. 'My soul is always in my hand; therefore will I not forget Thy law.' This morning, early, Mr. Oglethorpe called me out to tell me of Mrs. Lawley's miscarriage, by being denied access to the Doctor for bleeding. He seemed very angry, and to charge me with it; saying he should be the tyrant if he passed by such intolerable injuries. I answered I knew nothing of the matter, and it was hard it should be imputed to me; that from the first Hermsdorf told the Doctor he might visit whom of his patients he pleased; but the Doctor would not. I denied my having the least hand in the whole business, as Hermsdorf himself had declared. He said, 'Hermsdorf himself assured me, what he did, he did by your advice.' I answered, 'You must mistake his imperfect English; for many have heard him say the contradictory of this. Yet I must be charged with all the mischief.' 'How else can it be,' said he, 'that there should be no love, no meekness, no true religion among the people? but instead of that, mere formal prayers. As to that, I can answer for them that they have no more of the form of godliness than the power. I have seldom above six at the public service. 'But what would an unbeliever say to your raising these disorders?' 'Why, if I had raised them, he might say there was nothing in religion; but what would that signify to those who had experienced it? They would not say so.' He told me the people were full of dread and confusion; that it was much easier to govern a thousand than sixty men; for in so small a number, every one's passion was considerable; that he durst not leave them before they were settled, &c. I asked him, 'Would you have me forbear conferring at all with my parishioners?' To this I could get no answer,

14

and went on: 'The reason why I did not interpose for or against the Doctor was his having, at the beginning, charged me with his confinement. I talked less with my parishioners these five days past than I had done in any one afternoon before. I shunned appearing in public, lest my advice should be asked, or lest, if I heard others talking, my very silence should be deciphered into advice. But one argument of my innocence I can give, which will even convince you of it. I know my life is in your hands: and you know, that was you to frown upon me, and give the least intimation that it would be agreeable to you, the generality of these wretched people would say or swear any thing.' To this he agreed, and owned the case was so with them all. 'You see that my safety depends on your single opinion of me. Must I not therefore be mad, if I would in such a situation provoke you by disturbing the public peace? Innocence, I know, is not the least protection; but my sure trust is in God.' Here company interrupted us, and I left him.

I was no longer careful of the event after reading those words in the morning lesson: 'Thou canst not follow Me now; but thou shalt follow Me afterwards.' (John xiii. 36.) Amen. When Thou pleasest. Thy time is best.

Mr. Oglethorpe, meeting me in the evening, asked when I had prayers. I said, I waited his pleasure. While the people came slowly, 'You see, sir,' said I, 'they do not lay too great a stress on forms.' 'The reason of that is because others idolize them.' 'I believe few stay away for that reason.' 'I don't know that.' Mr. Oglethorpe stood over against me, and joined audibly in the prayers. The chapter was designed for me, and I read it with great boldness, as follows: 'I charge thee before God, and the Lord Jesus Christ, who shall judge the quick and the dead at His appearing and His kingdom; preach the word; be instant in season, out of season; reprove, rebuke, exhort with all long-suffering and doctrine. For the time will come when they will not endure sound doctrine.' 'But watch thou in all things, endure afflictions, do the work of an evangelist, make full proof of thy ministry.' 'At my first answer no man stood with me, but all men forsook me.' 'Notwithstanding the Lord stood with me ... that by me the preaching might be fully known, and that all the Gentiles might hear: and I was delivered out of the mouth of the lion. And the Lord shall deliver me from every evil work, and will preserve me unto His heavenly kingdom: to whom be glory for ever and ever. Amen.' (2 Tim. iv. 1-3, 5, 16-8.)

Saturday, March 27. This morning we began our Lord's last discourses to His disciples: every word was providentially directed to my comfort, but particularly those: 'Let not your heart be troubled: ye believe in God, believe also in Me.' 'I will not leave you comfortless: I will come to you.' 'Peace I leave with you, My peace I give unto you. Let not your heart be troubled, neither let it be afraid.' (John xiv. 1, 18, 27.)

I was sensibly concerned this afternoon at hearing that Mrs. Welch is growing more and more like Mrs. Hawkins, declares she will be no longer priest-ridden, jests upon prayers, and talks in the loose, scandalous dialect of her friend. In the evening a thought came into my mind of sending Mr. Ingham for my brother. He was much averse to leaving me in my trials, but was at last persuaded to go.

Sunday, March 28. I went to the storehouse (our tabernacle at present) to hearken what the Lord God would say concerning me. Both myself and the congregation were struck with the first lesson: Joseph and Potiphar's wife. The second was still more animating: 'If the world hate you, ye know that it hated Me before it hated you. If ye were of the world, the world would love his own.' (John xv. 18, 19.) After the prayers poor Mr. Davison stayed behind, to take his leave of Mr. Ingham. He burst into tears, and said: 'One good man is leaving us already. I foresee nothing but desolation. Must my poor children be brought up like these savages?' We endeavoured to comfort him by showing him his calling. At ten Mr. Ingham preached an alarming sermon on the day of judgement, and joined with me in offering up the Christian sacrifice.

In my walk at noon I was full of heaviness; complained to God that I had no friend but Him; and even in Him could now find no comfort. Immediately I received power to pray; then, opening my Bible, read as follows: 'Hearken unto Me, ye that seek the Lord: look unto the rock whence ye are hewn.' 'Fear ye not the reproach of men, neither be ye afraid of their revilings.' 'Who art thou, that thou shouldest be afraid of a man that shall die; ...and hast feared continually every day because of the fury of the oppressor? and where is the fury of the oppressor?' (Isa. li. 1, 2, 12, 13.) After reading this, no wonder that I found myself renewed in confidence.

While Mr. Ingham waited for the boat, I took a turn with Mr. Horton. He fully convinced me of Mrs. Hawkins's true character: ungrateful in the highest degree, a common prostitute, a complete hypocrite. He told me her husband and she had begged him upon their knees to intercede with Mr. Oglethorpe not to turn them out of the ship, which would be their utter ruin. This he accordingly did; though Mr. Oglethorpe at first assured him he had rather given one hundred pounds than take them. The first person she fell upon, after this, was Mr. Horton himself, whom she abused as she has since done me. From him I hastened to the water-side, where I found Mr. Ingham just put off. happy, happy friend! *Abiit, erupit, evasit!* But woe is me, that I am still constrained to dwell with Meshech! I languished to bear him company, followed him with my eyes till out of sight, and then sunk into deeper dejection than I had known before.

Monday, March 29. I was revived by those words of our Lord: 'These things have I spoken unto you, that you should not be offended. They shall put you out of the synagogues: yea, the time cometh, that whosoever killeth you will think that he doeth God service. And these things will they do unto you, because they have not known the Father, nor Me.' 'In the world ye shall have tribulation: but be of good cheer; I have overcome the world.' (John xvi. 1-3, 33.)

16

Knowing I was to live with Mr. Oglethorpe, I had brought nothing with me from England, except my clothes and books; but this morning, asking a servant for something I wanted (I think a tea-kettle), I was told Mr. Oglethorpe had given orders that no one should use any of his things. I answered, that order, I supposed, did not extend to me. 'Yes, sir,' says she, 'you was excepted by name.' Thanks be to God that it is not yet made capital to give me a morsel of bread.

Tuesday, March 30. Having laid hitherto on the ground, in a corner of Mr. Reed's hut, and hearing some boards were to be disposed of, I attempted in vain to get some of them to lie upon. They were given to all besides. The minister only of Frederica must be ἀφρήτωρ, ἀθέμιστος, ἀνέστιος. Yet are we not hereunto called, ἀστατεῖν κακοπαθεῖν. Even the Son of Man had not where to lay His head!

I find the Scripture an inexhaustible fund of comfort. 'Is My hand shortened at all, that it cannot save? or have I no power to deliver? ... I gave my back to the smiters, and my cheeks to them that plucked off the hair. I hid not my face from shame and spitting. For the Lord God will help me, therefore shall I not be confounded. Therefore have I set my face like a flint; and I know that I shall not be ashamed. He is near that justifieth me; who will contend with me? Let us stand together. Who is mine adversary? let him come near to me. Behold, the Lord God will help me: who is he that shall condemn me?'

Wednesday, March 31. I begin now to be abused and slighted into an opinion of my own considerableness. I could not be more trampled upon, was I a fallen Minister of State. The people have found out that I am in disgrace, and all the cry is:

> *Curramus praecipites, et*
> *Dum jacit in ripa calcemus Caesaris hostem.*

My few well-wishers are afraid to speak to me. Some have turned out of the way to avoid me. Others desired I would not take it ill if they seemed not to know me when we should meet. The servant that used to wash my linen sent it back unwashed. It was great cause of triumph my being forbid the use of Mr. Oglethorpe's things, and in effect debarred of most of the conveniences, if not necessaries, of life. I sometimes pitied and sometimes diverted myself with the odd expressions of their contempt; but found the benefit of having undergone a much lower degree of obloquy at Oxford.

Thursday, April 1. In the midst of morning service a poor scoutboat-man was brought in, who was almost killed by the burst of a cannon. I found him senseless and dying. All I could do was to pray for him and try by his example to wake his two companions. He languished till the next day, and died.

Hitherto I have been borne up by a spirit not my own; but exhausted nature at last prevails. It is amazing she held out so long. My outward hardships and inward conflicts, the bitterness of reproach from the only man I wished to please,

> At last have worn my boasted courage down.

Accordingly, this afternoon, I was forced by a friendly fever to take my bed. My sickness, I knew, could not be of long continuance; but, as I was in want of every help and convenience, must either shortly leave me or release me from farther suffering.

In the evening Mrs. Hird and Mrs. Robinson called to see me, and offered me all the assistance in their power. I thanked them, but desired they would not prejudice themselves by taking this notice of me. At that instant we were alarmed with a cry of the Spaniards being come; heard many guns fired and saw the people fly in great consternation to the Fort. I felt not the least disturbance or surprise; bade the women not fear, for God was with us. Within a few minutes news was brought us that the alarm was only a contrivance of Mr. Oglethorpe, to try the people. My charitable visitants then left me, and soon returned with some gruel, which threw me into a sweat. The next morning, April 2, they ventured to call again. At night, when my fever was somewhat abated, I was led out to bury the scoutboat-man, and envied him his quiet grave.

Saturday, April 3. Nature I found endeavoured to throw off the disease by excessive sweats: I therefore drank whatever my women brought me.

Sunday, April 4. Many of the people had been ill of the bloody flux. I escaped hitherto by my vegetable diet; but now my fever brought it. Notwithstanding this, I was obliged to go abroad, and preach, and administer the sacrament. My sermon on 'Keep innocency, and take heed to the thing that is right, for this shall bring a man peace at the last,' was deciphered into a satire against Mrs. Hawkins. At night I got an old bedstead to lie on, being that on which the scoutboat-man had died.

Monday, April 5. At one this morning the sandflies forced me to rise, and smoke them out of the hut. The whole town was employed in the same manner. My congregation in the evening consisted of two Presbyterians and a Papist. I went home in great pain, my distemper being much increased with the little duty I could discharge.

Tuesday, April 6. I found myself so faint and weak, that it was with the utmost difficulty I got through the prayers. Mr. Davison, my good Samaritan, would often call, or send his wife to tend me: and to their care, under God, I owe my life.

To-day Mr. Oglethorpe gave away my bedstead from under me, and refused to spare one of the carpenters to mend me up another.

Friday, April 9. While talking to Mrs. Hird, I turned my eyes towards the huts, and saw Mr. Lassel's all in a blaze. I walked towards the fire, which before I could come up to it had consumed the hut and everything in it. It was a corner hut, and the wind providentially blew from the others, or they would have been all destroyed.

Saturday, April 10. Mr. Reed waked me with news of Mr. Delamotte and my brother being on their way to Frederica. I found the encouragement I sought in the Scriptures for the day, Psalm liii.: 'Why boastest thou thyself in mischief, mighty man? the goodness of God endureth continually. Thy tongue deviseth mischiefs; like a sharp razor, working deceitfully. Thou lovest evil more than good; and lying than to speak righteousness.' At six Mr. Delamotte and my brother landed, when my strength was so exhausted I could not have read prayers once more. He helped me into the woods; for there was no talking among a people of spies and ruffians; nor even in the woods, unless in an unknown tongue. He told me the Scripture he met with at landing was, 'If God be for us, who can be against us?' and that Mr. Oglethorpe received him with abundant kindness. I began my account of all that has passed, and continued it till prayers. It were endless to mention all the Scriptures which have been for so many days adapted to my circumstances; but I cannot pass by the evening lesson, Heb. xi. I was ashamed of having well-nigh sunk under mine, when I beheld the conflicts of those triumphant sufferers, of whom the world was not worthy.

Sunday, April 11. What words could more support our confidence than the following, out of the Psalms for the day? 'Be merciful unto me, God, for man goeth about to devour me. He is daily fighting, and troubling me. Mine enemies are daily in hand to swallow me up; for they be many that fight against me, O thou Most Highest. Nevertheless, though I am sometimes afraid, yet put I my trust in Thee. I will put my trust in God, and will not fear what man can do unto me. They daily mistake my words: all that they imagine is to do me evil.' (Ps. lvi. 1-5.) The next Psalm was equally animating: 'Be merciful unto me, O God; for my soul trusteth in Thee: and under the shadow of Thy wings shall be my refuge, until this tyranny be overpast. I will call upon the most high God; even unto the God that shall perform the cause which I have in hand. He shall send down from heaven, and save me from the reproof of him that would eat me up. God shall send forth His mercy and truth; my soul is among lions. And I lie even among the children of men, that are set on fire: whose teeth are spears and arrows, and their tongue a sharp sword. Set up thyself, O God, above the heavens; and thy glory above all the earth.' (Ps. lvii. 1-6.)

I had just recovered strength enough to consecrate at the sacrament: the rest my brother discharged. We then got out of the reach of informers, and proceeded in my account; being fully persuaded of the truth of Mrs. Welch's information against Mr. Oglethorpe, Mrs. Hawkins, and herself.

Next morning Mr. Oglethorpe met and carried us to breakfast at the modest Mrs. Hawkins's. At noon my brother repeated to me his last conference with Mrs. Welch, in confirmation of all she had ever told me.

At night I took leave of Mr. Horton, Mr. Hermsdorf, and Major Richards, who were going with thirty men to build a fort over against the Spanish lookout, twelve leagues from Augustine.

Wednesday, April 14. By a relation which my brother gave me of a late conference he had with her, I was, in spite of all I had seen and heard, half-persuaded into a good opinion of Mrs. Hawkins. For the lasting honour of our sagacity be it written!

Friday, April 16. My brother brought me off a resolution, which honour and indignation had formed, of starving rather than ask for necessaries. Accordingly I went to Mr. Oglethorpe, in his tent, to ask for some little things I wanted. He sent for me back again, and said, 'Pray, sir, sit down. I have something to say to you. I hear you have spread several reports about me and Mrs. Hawkins. In this you are the author of them. There is a great difference in telling such things to another and to me. In you who told it your brother, tis scandal; in him who repeated it to me, 'tis friendship. My religion does not, like the Pharisees', consist in long prayers, but in for giving injuries, as I do this of yours, not but that the thing is in itself a trifle and hardly deserves a serious answer; though I gave one to your brother because he believed the report true. 'Tis not such things as these which hurt my character. They would pass for gallantries and rather recommend me to the world.'

[Here he made slight of the matter, at the same time vindicating himself from the imputations, and went on: 'I know many suppose a thirst of fame the motive of all my actions, but they are mistaken. I have had more than my share of it, and my fortune is now, I believe, on the turn.'

After lifting up my heart to God I replied: 'I come first (Note: He means, I come to the first point.); and as you suppose me guilty, 'tis the greatest kindness that you can forgive me. I shall only speak the truth and leave you to judge of it. I absolutely deny the whole charge. I have neither raised nor spread this report, but wherever I heard it, checked it immediately. Some who themselves spoke it in my hearing have, I suppose, gone, and fathered their own words upon me. I had myself mentioned this to you, had I still continued in your favour. I did mention it to my brother, that he might tell it you. Sup pose I myself believed it, I should never have propagated (it), because I am not to speak evil of the ruler of my people. The ground of the people's supposition was Mrs. Hawkins's great assurance during her confinement. All they say of you they say of my brother and her. She said so herself, at first, but has since eaten her words. The letter she intercepted was wrote before this report was heard of. I own, to suffer thus as an evildoer, and from you, is the severest trial I have ever known. My shyness was caused by yours. As I shall always think it my duty to please you to the utmost of my power, I hope you will look upon me as you used to do. I know your unforgiving temper, and that if you once entertain a suspicion or dislike, it is next to impossible to remove it.' He promised to be the same to me as before.

[At night Mrs. Welch sent for my brother. He being engaged with Mr. Oglethorpe, I went, and found her half dead with fear. She began accusing me of betraying her.

['Be not imposed upon; your betraying me shall never make me betray you.'

['But he will get it out of your brother.'

['No, my brother is a Christian; I am so much of one to prefer any sufferings to breaking my promise.'

[At ten I related this conversation to my brother. He then gave me a surprising account of Mr. Oglethorpe. Oh that it were true! Who knows but he may be innocent? God. God make and keep us all so! The Spaniards, he informed my brother, were expected every moment, and was himself in a calm expectation of death.

[*Saturday, April* 17. I called on Mrs. Welch, and asked what Mr. Oglethorpe had said last night. 'He again charged me with having told you, and therefore your brother: said I was in love with him, which I owned, but not as he thought. I told him he was all made up of art. He was exceeding sad when he left me.'

['Mrs. Welch, you have deeply injured me. I never built upon Mr. Oglethorpe's friendship, for I have no worldly expectations. But you have turned my best friend into an enemy for life. When in the openness of my heart I warned you against that very woman, how could you go immediately and betray me to her? Why would you even invent falsehoods to hurt me, and say to her and Mr. Oglethorpe that I raised the report about them? Did I deserve this at your hands? Was this gratitude?'

['No; very far from it. I know not what I meant; I was mad, I was out of my senses. But I beg you would not say anything to Mr. Oglethorpe.'

['No; you are safe. I cannot return evil for evil. But I must in justice tell Mr. Oglethorpe 'twas not I informed you, but you informed me of the scandalous reports. But what was your end in saying what you did of Mrs. Hawkins?'

['Oh, do not ask me. I was mad, I was be witched. I said I don't know what.'

['But was that false which you told us of your self?'

['It was. I never saw Mr. Oglethorpe till I came into the ship.'

['What end had you in vilifying yourself?'

['Do not ask me; I cannot tell.'

['Then I will for you. Answer me sincerely. Are you not in love with Mr. Oglethorpe? and did you not invent all these falsehoods to gain credit with my brother and thereby employ him to throw out Mrs. Hawkins, and so make room for yourself?'

['You say the very thing; 'tis so.'

[An hour after, I was with her again, and in formed her I intended to set Mr. Oglethorpe right, as she in justice to me ought to have done. She replied: 'I have been almost distracted at the thoughts of my treatment of you; that I should incense Mr. Oglethorpe to such a devilish outrage; that I should be the devil's instrument in crushing you, in destroying the innocent. The devil surely was in me. I raised Mr. Oglethorpe's suspicions of you. I complained of your being so troublesome to me. I accused you against my conscience of a base design, and have estranged him from you entirely.'

['How had I provoked you to it? Did you ever receive aught but good from me?'

['No; but Mrs. Hawkins was continually in citing me to it, saying, "We must supplant these parsons, and then we shall have Mr. Oglethorpe to ourselves. Do you accuse Charles Wesley to him, and I will accuse the other." I hear she said that of your brother which I said of you. I am not sure, but find she has laid all upon me, and would have me ruin you, that she may ruin me.'

['Then what you said of her history to my brother is true again?'

['Every word of it. Her design of drawing him on and then exposing him, with all the account I gave your brother, is true.'

[Upon her again falling into self-condemnation, I said, 'God forgive you as freely as I do. You owe me a public vindication, but my innocence shall surely meet with the fullest vindication from God.'

[I related to my brother this conversation, and we were both utterly confounded.

[Soon after I got some time for meditation on death, and felt an hope of being accepted through Christ.]

The next day [April 18] my brother and Mr. Delamotte set out in an open boat for Savannah. I preached in the afternoon on 'He that now goeth on his way weeping, and beareth forth good seed, shall doubtless come again with joy, and bring his sheaves with him.'

Easter Eve, April 24. At ten I was sent for by Mr. Oglethorpe. He began: 'Mr. Wesley, you know what has passed between us. I took some pains to satisfy your brother about the reports concerning me, but in vain. He here renews his suspicions in writing. I did desire to convince him, because I had an esteem for him; and he is just so considerable to me as my esteem makes him. I could clear up all, but it matters not. You will soon see the reason of my actions.

'I am now going to death. You will see me no more. Take this ring, and carry it from me to Mr. V[ernon, one of the trustees of the colony]. If there is a friend to be depended upon, he is one. His interest is next to Sir Robert's. Whatever you ask, within his power, he will do for you, your brother, and your family. I have expected death for some days. These letters show that the Spaniards have long been seducing our allies, and intend to cut us off at a blow. I fall by my friends; Gascoin, whom I have made; the Carolina people, whom I depended upon to send their promised succours. But death is to me nothing. T. will pursue all my designs; and to him I recommend them and you.'

He then gave me a diamond ring: I took it, and said: 'If, as I believe,

Postremum fato, quod te alloquor, hoc est,

hear what you will quickly know to be true, as soon as you are entered upon the separate state. This ring I shall never make any use of for myself. I have no worldly hopes. I have renounced the world. Life is bitterness to me. I came hither to lay it down. You have been deceived, as well as I. I protest my innocence as to the crimes I am charged with; and take myself to be now at liberty to tell you what I thought never to have uttered. [Mrs. Welch excited in me the first suspicion of you after we were come here. She afterwards told you her own words as if they had been mine. This she confessed both to my brother and me, as likewise that she had falsely accused me to you of making love to her. She was put upon it by Mrs. Hawkins saying, "Let us supplant those parsons, and we shall have Mr. Oglethorpe to ourselves."]'

When I had finished this relation he seemed entirely changed, full of his old love and confidence in me. After some expressions of kindness, I asked him, 'Are you satisfied?' He replied, 'Yes, entirely.' 'Why then, sir, I desire nothing more upon earth; and care not how soon I follow you.' He added, he much desired the conversion of the heathen, and believed my brother intended for it. 'But I believe,' said I, 'it will never be under your patronage; for then men would account for it without taking in God.' He replied, 'I believe so too'; then embraced and kissed me with the most cordial affection. I attended him to the scout-boat, where he waited some minutes for his sword. They brought him first, and a second time, a mourning sword. At last they gave him his own, which had been his father's. 'With this sword,' says he, 'I was never yet unsuccessful.' 'I hope, sir,' said I, 'you carry with you a better, even the sword of the Lord, and of Gideon.' 'I hope so too,' he added.

When the boat put off, I ran before into the woods, to see my last of him. Seeing me and two others running after him, he stopped the boat, and asked whether we wanted anything. Captain Mackintosh, left Commander, desired his last orders. I then said, 'God be with you. Go forth, *Christo duce, et auspice Christo!*' 'You have,' says he, 'I think, some verses of mine. You there see my thoughts of success.' His last word to the people was, 'God bless you all!' The boat then carried him out of sight. I interceded for him, that God would save him from death, would wash out all his sins, and prepare, before He took, the sacrifice to Himself.

Easter Day, April 25. The people were alarmed at night by the sight of two great fires, on either side of the town, not knowing if they were made by friends or enemies. Next morning news was brought of a boat coming up Every one seemed under a consternation, though no one but myself was fully apprised of our dangers. At night the watch was doubled by Captain Mackintosh. The people being unwilling to comply with his orders, I was forced to tell Mr. Hird, the constable, that there might be danger which Mackintosh alone knew of, and therefore they ought to obey. He promised it for himself and the rest. Though I expected every hour that the Spaniards would bring us the news of Mr. Oglethorpe's death, yet I was insensible of fear, and careless of the consequence. But my indifference arose from stupidity rather than faith. There was nothing I cared for in life, and therefore the loss of it appeared a trifle.

Thursday, April 29. About half-hour past eight I went down to the bluff to see a boat coming up. At nine it arrived with Mr. Oglethorpe. I blessed God for still holding his soul in life. In the evening we took a walk together, and he informed me more particularly of our past danger. Three great ships, and four smaller, had been seen for three weeks together at the mouth of the river; but the wind continuing full against them, [they] were kept from making a descent, till they could stay no longer. I gave him back his ring, and said, 'I need not, sir, and indeed I cannot, tell you how joyfully and thank fully I return this.' 'When I gave it you,' said he, 'I never expected to receive it again, but thought it would be of service to your brother and you. I had many omens of my death, particularly their bringing me my mourning sword; but God has been pleased to preserve a life which was never valuable to me; and yet in the continuance of it, I thank God, I can rejoice.' 'I am now glad of all that has happened here, since without it I could never have had such a proof of your affection as that you gave me, when you looked upon me as the most ungrateful of villains. While I was speaking this he appeared full of tenderness; and passed on to observe the strangeness of his deliverance, when betrayed on all sides, without human support, and utterly defenceless. He condemned himself for his anger (God forgive those who made me the object of it!), which he imputed to his want of time for consideration. 'I longed, sir, to see you once more, that I might tell you some things before we finally parted; but then I considered that if you died, you would know them all in a moment.' 'I know not whether separate spirits regard our little concerns. If they do, it is as men regard the follies of their childhood, or as I my late passionateness.'

Friday, April 30. I had some farther talk with him in bed. He ordered me whatever he could think I wanted; promised to have me an house built immediately; and was just the same to me he had formerly been.

Sunday, May 2. I went to him to ask if there was any truth in the report that Major Richards and Mr. Horton were detained at Augustine, and the men at St. George's run away. He told me he hoped that the gentlemen were well received; but the people had been frightened away by two soldiers bringing a civil proffer of refreshment; that thereupon the men mutinied, and obliged Captain Hermsdorf to quit the advanced post, and turn homeward, which he had done pursuant to Ferguson's advice; that he intended immediately to go in quest of them. In an hour's time he set out accordingly.

In the evening I endeavoured to convince Mr. Moore (as I had done some few besides) of Mr. Oglethorpe's innocency. He then read me a list of the officers that were to be; and who should be appointed head-bailiff but my dear friend the Doctor!

Monday, May 3. The people had observed that I was taken into favour again, which I found by their provoking civilities.

Wednesday, May 5. At night news was brought of a boat being seen off the point, which would not come to, though the soldiers had fired at her several times. The people were greatly alarmed, being in no preparation for an enemy. I went to bed, but was soon awakened by the firing of a gun; and, rising, found all the town flocking towards the fort, in the utmost consternation. I walked leisurely after them, without fear, yet without faith; found the uproar was occasioned by a friendly Indian; and walked back again.

Saturday, May 8. I had some affecting talk with a poor man, belonging to the scout-boat, who had broke his arm. He owned himself greatly moved by the *Christian Monitor* I had given him; convinced thereby of the truth of religion; unable to read for tears; and fully resolved to obey the motions of the Holy Spirit, by leading a new life.

Between ten and eleven I was waked again by an alarm. I rose, as did all the women, and found a signal had been made from the man-of-war. I sent away the women, and, being myself of equal service, soon followed their example, and went to sleep again.

Sunday, May 9. Notice was given me that Mr. Dison, Chaplain to the Independent Company, was landed, and walking toward me. His moral character did not recommend him. I had just time to run away into the woods, and so escaped his visit. The next morning Mr. Oglethorpe returned, from whom I had the following account of his expedition.

On *Saturday, May* 1, late at night, arrived the *Caroline* scout-boat, with Captain Ferguson, bringing advice that Major Richards and Mr. Horton (who had carried answers to the Spanish Governor's letters) had landed at their lookout, and he believed were made prisoners by the Spaniards; for they had heard no more of them, except by a blind letter, written with a pencil; that the boats, in which were the men under Captain Hermsdorf, were come about thirty miles on this side St. George's Point, and there waited for orders; that the men were mutinous, and Hermsdorf believed he should be forced to retire to Fort St. Andrews; that he was apprehensive they would either murder their officers, and turn pirates, or be cut off by the Spaniards. Mr. Oglethorpe, on Sunday, went on board the man-of-war, and proceeded from thence with the man-of-war's boat, commanded by the Lieutenant, and the Georgia scout-boat. They arrived that night at Fort St. Andrews. On Monday they came up with the south point of Cumberland, where we met with the boats under the command of Captain Hermsdorf. Mr. Oglethorpe immediately took them out to sea with him, round Amelia Island. He found, upon examination, that the men did not intend to mutiny; but that the suspicion was occasioned by the lies of one man, who was hereupon sentenced by Mr. Oglethorpe to run the gauntlet.

He went to Point St. George, within sight of the Spanish look-out, and resettled them on the same place where Mr. Hermsdorf had before taken up his quarters. It had been agreed that the Spaniards should make a signal; and from thence he would repair with his boats, to fetch Major Richards back, who was gone to Augustine, at the request of the Governor, who promised to send horses to conduct him, but did not. It likewise was agreed that the boats should patrol up and down the rivers, to prevent the Indians, our allies, passing over to molest the Spaniards; as they should prevent their Indians passing over to molest us.

Mr. Oglethorpe went that afternoon to the Spanish look-out, with a flag of truce; but not being able to perceive any one, leaving the boat at her grappling, he leaped ashore himself, to see if he could discover anybody there; and going along the beach, at a distance from the sandy hillocks, to prevent surprise, he surrounded the hillocks, where he found two horses hobbled. He went forward to a palmetto hut; but could find no man. After this he sent the flag of truce into a great savannah, to see if that would draw down any people to a conference. Upon this, W. Frazer, a Scotch lad, going into the neighbouring woods, and finding a Spaniard, brought him to Mr. Oglethorpe, to whom he delivered two letters; one from Major Richards, the other from Mr. Horton, directed to Mr. Hermsdorf, acquainting him that he should be back with him in two days time. Mr. Oglethorpe gave the man a bottle of wine, victuals, and tobacco, and a moidore for his trouble in bringing the letters; and inquired where Major Richards and Mr. Horton were. The man said he knew nothing concerning them; that he was an horseman, and sent by the Colonel of the cavalry from the head quarters, which were about twelve leagues off, with these letters, to wait there till he should see an English boat appear, and deliver it to them; that he had lain four days on the beach, and had not discovered a boat in that time. Mr. Oglethorpe delivered to him letters for the Governor of Augustine; and between ten and eleven on Thursday morning set out with the man-of-war's boat and Georgia scout-boat to meet the man again, according to appointment.

He discovered a guard-coast full of men, that lay behind the sand-bank, beyond the breakers, on the English side of the water; and soon after he discovered several men hid in the woods, next to some sand-hills. Two horsemen showed themselves, and beckoned to the boats, which had a flag of truce flying, to come down to a point beyond which the guard-coast lay concealed: on which Mr. Oglethorpe rowed with the two boats toward the guard-coast, that he might not leave her behind to intercept us and our people at St. George's Point.

There seemed to be about seventy men on board her, and there were in our boats twenty-four. She lay still for some time; but when they found plainly that they were discovered, they rowed away with incredible swiftness, directly out to sea, toward Augustine.

Mr. Oglethorpe returned to the horsemen, who seemed very unwilling to approach the boats, but at last agreed to receive a letter, if Mr. Oglethorpe would send an unarmed man ashore. One of them, seemingly an officer, forbade the boats to land on the King of Spain's ground. Mr. Oglethorpe answered, that as it was the King of Spain's ground, the English would forbear landing on it, since the Spaniards requested it; but that the Spaniards should be very welcome to land on the King of England's ground, which was on the opposite side of the river, and should be welcome to a glass of wine with him there. He asked him for the news of Mr. Horton and Mr. Richards, and whether he could not send anything to them. The man said he knew nothing of them; that he received his orders from the Colonel of horse, who was quartered at twelve leagues distance; and that he could carry no news but to him.

Upon this, Mr. Moore, Lieutenant of the *Hawk* man-of-war, wrote a letter to the Colonel of the horse, acquainting him that he was come thither with boats, to conduct back the gentlemen who were sent by Mr. Oglethorpe to treat with the Governor of Augustine; and that, if at any time he would make three fires on the Spanish main, he would take it as a signal that the gentlemen were come, and would come over with a boat and fetch them. The Spanish officer promised to deliver the letter by night to the Colonel of horse. Mr. Oglethorpe stayed till Saturday night, expecting an answer, and sent over to the Spanish side every day; but could find nobody to have conference with. By the look-out withinland they have a vineyard, flocks of turkeys, cattle, and horses; but great care was taken that none of our people should touch any of them. On Saturday night Mr. Oglethorpe set out, leaving Captain Hermsdorf with an armed periagua, (Note: Spanish, a canoe formed out of the trunk of a tree.) the Georgia scout-boat, and another boat.

Tuesday, May 11. I had now so far recovered my strength, that I could again expound the lesson. In the lesson next morning was Elisha encompassed with the host at Dothan. It is our privilege, as Christians, to apply those words to ourselves: There be more that be with us than those that be against us. God spoke to us yet plainer in the second lesson: Behold, I send you forth as sheep in the midst of wolves: be ye therefore wise as serpents, and harmless as doves. But beware of men: for they will deliver you up to the councils; ...and ye shall be brought before governors and kings for My sake. And ye shall be hated of all men for My name's sake: but he that endureth to the end shall be saved. But when they persecute you in this city, flee ye into another. The disciple is not above his master. Fear ye not therefore: for there is nothing covered, that shall not be revealed, and hid that shall not be known. (Matt. x. 16-26.) In explaining this, I dwelt on that blessed topic of consolation to the innocent, that however he suffers under a false accusation here, he will shortly be cleared at God's righteous bar, where the accuser and the accused shall meet face to face, and the guilty person acquit him whom he unjustly charged, and take back the wickedness to himself. Poor Mrs. Welch, who was just over against me, could not stand it, but first turned her back, and then retired behind the congregation.

While I waited for Mr. Oglethorpe, setting out again for the southward, Mr. Appee (Note: Charles Wesley afterwards found this young Dutchman to be an infidel, a libertine, a liar, and a thief.) accosted me, a young gentleman lately come from Savannah. He mentioned his desire of being baptized (having only received lay-baptism before). I thought he ought to have a longer trial of his own sincerity. He passed on to his intended marriage with Miss Bovey, which I dissuaded him from, not thinking either sufficiently prepared for it. He owned he had made little progress in subduing his will, and ought to be more dead to the world before he threw himself into it. Near midnight I took leave of Mr. Oglethorpe, who set out in the scout-boat, after the other boats, for St. George's. The remainder of the night I passed upon the ground in the guard-room.

At four the next day I set out for Savannah, whither the Indian traders were coming down to meet me, and take out licences. I was overjoyed at my deliverance out of this furnace, and not a little ashamed of myself for being so.

Sunday, May 16. We landed at Skidoway, and dined at Mrs. Mouse's. I then went round and asked the few people there were upon the island to come to prayers; which accordingly I read, and preached to about ten in the guard room; and promised so to contrive, if possible, that they should be supplied once a month.

At four we returned to our boat, and by six reached Thunderbolt; whence I walked the five remaining miles to Savannah. Mr. Ingham, Mr. Delamotte, and my brother were surprised at my unexpected visit; but it being late, we each retired to his respective corner of the room, where, without the help of a bed, we slept soundly till the morning.

Wednesday, May 19. According to our agreement, my brother set forward for Frederica, and I took charge of Savannah in his absence. The hardest duty imposed on me was the expounding the lesson morning and evening to one hundred hearers. I was surprised at my own confidence, and acknowledged it not my own. The day was usually divided between visiting my parishioners, considering the lesson, and conversing with Mr. Ingham, Delamotte, and Appee.

Tuesday, May 25. I visited a girl of fifteen, who lay a-dying of an incurable illness. She had been in that condition many months, as her parents, some of the best people of the town, informed me. I started at the sight of a breathing corpse. Never was real corpse half so ghastly. Her groans and screams alone distinguished her from one. They had no intermission; yet was she perfectly sensible, as appeared by her feebly lifting up her eyes when I bade her trust in God, and read the prayers for the energumens. We were all in tears. She made signs for me to come again.

Friday, May 28. Mr. Oglethorpe returned from the frontiers. The following account of his expedition I extracted out of his letter to the Trustees:

'After that flagrant breach of the law of nations, putting our messengers, sent with a flag of truce, under arrest, I could expect nothing but farther hostilities, and therefore prepared to repel force by force. We fortified, with the utmost speed that the smallness of our number would allow, St. George's Point, within sight of the Spanish outguards, and were much facilitated by finding the ruins of a fort built by Sir Francis Drake; so that we had nothing to do but to repair and palisade the breaches made by time, and to clear the ditches, which were originally thirty feet deep.

'The Independent Company and man-of-war being posted below Frederica, I drew out from thence, and from the Scotch settlements, what men I possibly could, to increase the garrison on St. George's Point. While we were getting down recruits and cannon, the Governor of Augustine, having before put our messengers under arrest, sent out Don Ignatio, Colonel of foot, with thirty of his picked men, some Yamasaw Indians, and a strong boat's crew, about sixty men, in a launch to reconnoiter our settlements; and, if he had found us so weak as the advices from Carolina said we were, to dislodge us. Don Ignatio came out by sea, and attempted to get undiscovered into Jekyl's Sound; was discovered by Ensign Delegall, who commanded a guard upon the sea-point. He hailed them to give an account who they were; which they refusing, he fired some cannon with powder; and about the same time they discovered the man-of-war lying within the sound. They ran out to sea with great precipitation, and strove to get in at another inlet, by the island of Cumberland; where the Scotch from St. Andrews challenged them. They neither answered nor hung out colours, but rowed away in such haste, that the same night they reached the Spanish outguards, on St. John's river, near sixty miles distant.

'Don Ignatio landed in the night, and had a conference with Don Pedro de Lamberti, the Commander of the Spanish horse; who was come up by land to the look-out, with one hundred and sixty foot, and fifty horse. They concluded by the two forts they had met with, and the man-of-war's being there, that all our strength lay at Frederica, and that we were weak at Fort St. George; therefore resolved to try to surprise some of our boats, and upon their intelligence leave their horses, carry over their men by water and attack us the night following. This was on Wednesday. I, having discovered some fires on the Spanish main, concluded troops came down, and therefore, in order to make them delay attacking us till our succours should arrive on Thursday morning, I had two carriage-guns, and two swivel-guns, which we had brought with us, carried into the woods, that the Spaniards might not distinguish where they were fired; and ordered the swivel-guns to be re-charged so often as to make a salute of seven, and with the carriage-guns fired five shot in answer. The swivel-guns, by reason of the smallness of the report, seemed like a ship at a distance saluting, and the carriage-guns like batteries answering from the shore.

'I set out with two boats, and a flag of truce, to meet the Spaniards. They concluded from the guns, as I have heard since, that there was a new strength arrived; in which they were confirmed by our boats rowing briskly toward them: on which their launch thought proper to make the best of their way toward Augustine. There the soldiers and boatmen, fatigued with over labour, spread such dismal accounts, magnifying our strength and diligence, in order to save their own reputation, that they created a general uproar among the people.

'That night I had several fires made in the woods, some at two, some at three, miles distance from Point St. George. On Friday morning the foot and horse, under the command of Don Pedro, finding themselves abandoned by the launch, and therefore in no possibility of passing over into the island against us; and from the many fires in the woods collecting that the Creek Indians were come up; having left a small guard of horse to observe our motions, retired in good order to Augustine. Their arrival doubled the confusion, they apprehending that if the Indians should cut off their communication by land, as the man-of-war might do by sea, they should perish by famine. The Governor was obliged to call a council of war, in which the oldest officers, and indeed almost all, gave their opinion that the gentlemen sent by me should be immediately released, and sent back in the most honourable manner, with an officer attending them, to treat with me, and desire me to restrain the Indians from invading them: at the same time to ask me why we settled upon lands and territories belonging to the King of Spain.

'Not knowing anything of these proceedings, except that the Spaniards were retired, I lay at Fort St. George from Thursday to Sunday; in which time fresh troops arrived: and falling all of us to work, with the officers and men of the King's troop, who distinguished themselves upon this occasion, we mounted some guns upon the batteries along the river and got the fortifications in good forwardness; and having left the fort under the command of Captain Hermsdorf, retired with the utmost diligence to Frederica.

'There I found the King of the Uchees, with thirty men, who offered to assist me with one hundred more against the Spaniards. King Tomo Chachi was also there, with thirty men, and an account that hundreds of the Creeks eagerly desired to fall upon the Spaniards. In three days I set out with a large periagua, and fifty men, cannon, and provision for two months, two ten-oared boats, and the Indians in their own boats, to relieve St. George, which I imagined by that time might be besieged. God was pleased to prosper us; so that about fifteen miles from St. George's, being fortunately an hour ahead of the rest of the boats, I met a Spanish boat, with a flag of truce flying, and Mr. Dempsey, and the gentlemen sent to Augustine in her, together with Don Pedro de Lamberti, Captain of their troop of horse, and Don Manuel, Secretary to the Governor, and Adjutant of the garrison. It was lucky the Indians were not foremost; for if they had been, they would certainly have engaged the Spanish boat; which, as it was, I could hardly prevent, by sending a ten-oared boat to guard them to Frederica. Then I ordered them to be received on board the man-of-war, where they dined with me. I received them with the greatest form I could, having a guard of the King's troops on the right hand, with their bayonets fixed; and on the left hand the Highlanders, with their targets, and broad-swords drawn.

'After dinner we drank the King of Britain's and the King of Spain's health, under the discharge of cannon from the ship; which was answered with fifteen pieces of cannon from Delegall's fort, at the sea-point. That again was followed by the cannon from the fort of St. Andrews, and that by those of Frederica and the Darien, as I had before ordered. The Spaniards seemed extremely surprised that there should be so many forts, and all within hearing of one another. Don Pedro smiled, and said, 'No wonder Don Ignatio made more haste home than out.' After the healths were done, a great number of Indians came on board, naked, painted, and their heads dressed in feathers. They demanded of me justice against the Spaniards, for having killed some of their men in time of full peace. They farther proved that after the woman was taken, she was abused by numbers of men; and when she had satisfied their lust for two days, they inhumanly burned her alive.

'Don Pedro, having asked several questions, acknowledged himself fully satisfied of the fact; excusing it by saying he was then in Mexico, and that the Governor, being newly come from Spain, and not knowing the customs of the country, had sent out Indians under the command of the Pohoia King of the Floridas, who had exceeded his orders, which were not to make war with the Creeks. But the Indians not being content with that answer, he undertook that, at his return to Augustine, he would have the Pohoia King put to death, if he could be taken; and if he could not, that the Spaniards would supply his people with neither powder, arms, nor anything else, but leave them to the Creeks. The Indians answered that he spake well; and if the Spaniards did what he said, all should be white between them; but if not, they would take revenge; from which, at my desire, they would abstain till a final answer came.

'The Indian matters being thus settled, we had a conference with the Spanish Commissioners. They thanked me first for my restraining the Indians who were in my power, and hoped I would extend that care to the upper Indians. They then, after having produced their credentials, presented a paper, the contents whereof were to know by what title I settled upon St. Simon's, being lands belonging to the King of Spain. I took the paper, promising an answer the next day. The substance was, that the lands belonged to the King of England by undoubted right; that I had proceeded with the utmost caution, having taken with me Indians, the natives, and possessors of those lands; that I had examined every place, to see if there were any Spanish possessions, and went forward till I found an outguard of theirs, over against which I settled the English, without committing any hostilities, or dislodging any. Therefore I did not extend the King's dominions, but only settled with regular garrisons that part of them which was before a shelter for Indians, pirates, and such sort of disorderly men.

'The rest of the evening we spent in conversation, which chiefly turned upon the convenience it would be, both to the Spaniards and English, to have regular garrisons in sight of each other. Don Pedro smiled, and said he readily agreed to that; and should like very well to have their Spanish guard upon the south side of H__ river (which is within five miles of Charlestown, and where the Spaniards had a garrison in King Charles the First's time). I replied, I thought it was better as it was; for there were a great many people living between who could never be persuaded to come into his sentiments. At last Don Pedro acquainted me that he thought the Spaniards would refer the settling of the limits to the courts of Europe: for which purpose he would write to their court; and in the mean time desired no hostilities might be committed, and that I would send up a Commissary to sign with the Government an agreement to this purpose. I thereupon appointed Mr. Dempsey to be my Commissary, and to return with them.

'Don Pedro is the ruling man in Augustine, and has more interest with the Council of War than the Governor. As he passed by St. George's Point, he sent a whole ox as a present to their garrison. He gave me some sweetmeats and chocolate. I gave him a gold watch, a gun, and fresh provisions. To Don Manuel I gave a silver watch, and sent back a boat to escort them. If the Spaniards had committed any hostilities, I could, by the help of the Indians, have destroyed Augustine with great facility. But God be praised, by His blessing, the diligence of Dempsey, and the prudence of Don Pedro, all bloodshed was avoided.

Saturday, May 29. At ten this evening I first met my traders, at Mr. Causton's, (Note: Mr. Causton was a prime mover in the persecution subsequently raised against Mr. John Wesley, which induced him to leave the colony. He had been convicted, both in England and in Georgia, of fraudulent practices in the application of public money.) the head bailiff; as I did some or other of them every day for some weeks.

Monday, May 31. About noon Mr. Oglethorpe sent us word that he was going to court. We went, and heard his speech to the people, in the close of which he said, 'If any one here has been abused or oppressed by any man, in or out of employment, he has free and full liberty of complaining. Let him deliver in his complaints in writing, at my house. I will read all over by myself, and do every particular man justice.'

At eight in the evening I waited upon him, and found the three magistrates, who seemed much alarmed by his speech, and hoped he would not discourage government. He dismissed them, and told me he feared his following my brother's advice, in hearing all complaints, would ruin the people; and he should never have any to serve him. I replied I thought the contrary; and that such liberty was the happiest thing that could happen to the colony, and much to be desired by all good men. He fell, I know not how, into talk of Frederica, and said:

['Your brother read me his diary, which astonished me to the last degree, and fully convinced me of your innocence. For if Mrs. Welch could so blacken me, she could you. I had intended, if she would have stood to her charge, to have sent for you and try you before all the people, pull off the mask, and punish you with the utmost severity, especially when I heard from your brother of your having defamed me with Mrs. Hawkins. I thought you a very devil, so to divert all inquiries into your own guilt by throwing the charge upon me! I had entirely excommunicated you from my little church within, and determined to make an example of you. Everything concurred to convince me of your guilt. All you did and said your very silence and shyness; your telling me you should be cut off from doing good to one half of your parishioners, if I did not vindicate you from Mrs. Hawkins's aspersions; your pretended tenderness for Mrs. Welch in the ship; your seeing her since, especially when your brother was here, running thither continually and staying till midnight, for I had you dogged for several days. All men would have condemned you upon your trial, the circumstances were so strong. And tried and sentenced you would infallibly have been, but that I considered the effect it would have upon religion. That that should be wounded through your side I could not bear. Your history would be made a play or novel of. The character you had in your former life, your coming here as missionary, would altogether have made as good a story as Madam Kevrs. These thoughts first staggered me; but above all, your uncle! (Note: Matthew Wesley, the London doctor.) His triumph over you and religion turned the scale; and I verily believe God sent me that night to be insulted by him, to save you.'

['But what did you think of my former life, and of my end in coming here?'

['I thought you was then sincere; but never meeting with any woman before, and being perhaps sometimes encouraged and sometimes checked by an artful woman, was drawn on unawares into such depths of wickedness, and was now wholly given up and abandoned to the power of the devil.'

['But my guilt would never have been believed by my friends in England.'

['The good who did believe it would think you fell as Sinton Barsissa.'

[I said among other things: 'The reason of my shyness was the opinion I had entertained of you from Mrs. Welch's account, which I am now at liberty to mention, since you know it all, in great measure from my brother. I thought you as very a devil as you thought me. The character she had given me of you was, if possible, worse than mine. She knew three of your mistresses in England. She was herself seduced by you, so was also Mrs. Hawkins. You believed no more of Christianity than Mahomet; was a truly wicked man, and in tended to take away my life. I expected no other for many days, never hoping to come alive from Frederica. What freed me at once from all anxiety was a word of Scripture, "Thou canst not follow Me now, but thou shalt follow Me hereafter."'

[He then assured me of his firm belief of the Christian revelation, 'which alone,' said he, 'has tied my hands, and prevented me from putting an end to a miserable life.'

['But when,' said I, 'did you first begin to suspect that I might be innocent?'

[He answered: 'Not till I went to the southward, as I thought upon certain death. For upon your saying in my tent: "If you can believe this you must think me a most complete villain." Alas! thought I, you well know what a villain I ought to think you.'

['What was it at last that convinced you of the contrary?'

['A dream made the first impression upon me, while I was sleeping in a boat towards the south wards. The manner is not all exact; but I never knew a dream deceive me. I thought you came to me and said something which quite convinced me of your innocence. This, when I awoke, put me upon reconsidering everything. What sprung the first doubt was what I had observed from the beginning, that Mrs. Welch was an exceedingly subtle woman. Next her telling me the story of you, and stopping short when she observed me, as she thought, not sufficiently forward to destroy you.'

['But you told me just as you went to the southwards, that you was satisfied.'

['I did so, and I was satisfied then, at least of your being penitent.'

['Did what I said conduce to it?'

['No; 'twas your looks, so sad, so pale and mortified! that I could not but say in myself, This man must either be innocent, or deeply penitent; whichever 'tis, 'tis the same to me. I am going to cast myself on death and the mercy of God, and shall I refuse forgiveness to my fellow creature? No, I will not only forgive him, but so forgive him as I would God should forgive me; leave him entirely acquitted and satisfied. All this I tell you that you may give God the glory, and beware of men. But I did not tell it your brother. Pride, I own, hindered me, lest my relating what Mrs. Welch had said of you immediately upon his telling me what she had said of me might look like retaliation. A second reason was my regard for him; for he would doubt my having entirely renounced my ill opinion of you; and as to what is past, though he forgive, he will never forget it. You, I am satisfied, would be tender of the poor unhappy woman, as I was, leaving her full of comfort. I am determined never to mention any word of all this to her, and desire you will not.'

['That I can readily promise, for my intercourse with her is over. I am no longer obliged to look upon her as one of my charge, and shall never speak to her of this matter. Indeed, my caution in conversing with her did not spring from any fear of these consequences, but from an advice of S. Spangenberg's, "never to talk with a woman without a witness, or in the face of the sun." I followed his directions; but did not see the providential reason of it until now.']

Sunday, June 6. I passed good part of this as of every day in conversing with Mr. Appee, who generally breakfasted and supped at our house. The subject of our discourse was my intention of resigning my place, which I resolved to do after my last conference with Mr. Oglethorpe. The giving up my salary and certain hopes of preferment weighed nothing against my resolution. I made Mr. Appee a proffer of them, which he did not accept, being obliged to return, to look after his fortune in Holland.

Tuesday, June 8. I was present at court, and heard the accusations against Mr. Causton, who stood by while Parker, the first tribune of the people, on whom the malcontents had built all their hopes, brought the heaviest charges I suppose that could be brought against him. But they were so incredible, trifling, and childish, that I thought them a full vindication of the magistrates, and admired Mr. Oglethorpe's patience in hearing them.

Wednesday, June 16. This and many fore going days have been mostly spent in drawing up bonds and affidavits, licences and instructions, for the traders; the evenings in writing letters for Mr. Oglethorpe. We seldom parted till midnight. To-night, at half-hour past twelve, he set out in the scout-boat for

Frederica. I went to bed at one, and rose again at four; but found no effect this variety of fatigue had upon my body till some time after.

Sunday, June 20. Walking in the Trustees' garden, I met the Miss Boveys, whom I had never been in company with. I found some inclination to join them; but it was a very short-lived curiosity.

Saturday, June 26. Mr. Oglethorpe and my brother returned from Frederica.

Thursday, July 1. I was at court while the Creek Indians had an audience with Mr. Oglethorpe; which I took down (as several afterwards) in short-hand.

Wednesday, July 7. Between four and five this morning Mr. Delamotte and I went into the Savannah. We chose this hour for bathing both for the coolness and because the alligators were not stirring so soon. We heard them indeed snoring all around us; and one very early riser swam by within a few yards of us. On Friday morning we had hardly left our usual place of swimming, when we saw an alligator in possession of it. Once afterwards Mr. Delamotte was in great danger; for an alligator rose just behind him, and pursued him to the land, whither he narrowly escaped.

Saturday, July 10. I was waked by the news my brother brought us, of Miss Bovey's sudden death. (See John Wesley's *Journal,* July 6-8, 1736.) It called up all my sorrow and envy. Ah, poor Ophelia! was continually in my mind, I thought thou shouldst have been my Hamlet's wife. Mr. Appee was just set out for Charlestown, [on his way to] Holland, intending to return, when he had settled his affairs, and marry her.

> But death had quicker wings than love.

The following evening I saw her in her coffin, and soon after in her grave.

Wednesday, July 21. I heard by my brother that I was to set sail in a few days for England.

Thursday, July 22. To-day I got their licences signed by Mr. Oglethorpe, countersigned them myself, and so entirely washed my hands of the traders.

Sunday, July 25. I resigned my secretary's place, in a letter to Mr. Oglethorpe. After prayers he took me aside, and asked me whether all I had said was not summed up in the line he showed me on my letter:

> *Magis apta tuis tua dona relinquo.*

> Sir, to yourself your slighted gifts I leave,
> Less fit for me to take, than you to give.

I answered, I desired not to lose his esteem, but could not preserve it with the loss of my soul. He answered, he was satisfied of my regard for him; owned my argument drawn from the heart unanswerable; and yet, said he, 'I would desire you not to let the Trustees know your resolution of resigning. There are many hungry fellows ready to catch at the office; and in my absence I cannot put in one of my own choosing. The best I can hope for is an honest Presbyterian, as many of the Trustees are such. Perhaps they may send me a bad man; and how far such a one may influence the traders and obstruct the reception of the gospel among the heathen, you know. I shall be in England before you leave it. Then you may either put in a deputy or resign.

'You need not be detained in London above three days; and only speak to some of my particular friends (Vernon, Hutchinson, and Towers), to the Board of Trustees, when called upon, and the Board of Trade.

'On many accounts I should recommend to you marriage, rather than celibacy. You are of a social temper, and would find in a married state the difficulties of working out your salvation exceedingly lessened, and your helps as much increased.'

Monday, July 26. The words which concluded the lesson, and my stay in Georgia, were, 'Arise, let us go hence.' Accordingly at twelve I took my final leave of Savannah. When the boat put off I was surprised that I felt no more joy in leaving such a scene of sorrows.

July 31. I arrived with my brother at Charlestown. I lay that night at an inn. Next morning I was much rejoiced at hearing Mr. Appee was still in town, waiting for my company to England. His ingenuous, open temper, and disengagement from the world, made me promise myself a very improving and agreeable voyage: especially as I doubted not but the sudden death of his mistress had taken off that appearance of lightness, which I attributed rather to his youth and education than any natural inconstancy. After break fasting with Mr. Eveley, a merchant who had bespoke lodgings for us, I went in quest of my friend. We met with equal satisfaction on both sides; but I did not observe those deep traces of sorrow and seriousness which I expected. I asked him whether his loss had had its due effect, in making his heart more tender and susceptible of divine impressions. By his answer I concluded his heart was right, and its uppermost desire was to recover the divine image.

Something of this desire I felt myself at the holy sacrament, and found myself encouraged, by an unusual hope of pardon, to strive against sin.

Monday, August 2. I had observed much, and heard more, of the cruelty of masters towards their negroes; but now I received an authentic account of some horrid instances thereof. The giving a child a slave of its own age to tyrannize over, to beat and abuse out of sport, was, I myself saw, a common practice. Nor is it strange, being thus trained up in cruelty, they should after wards arrive at so great perfection in it; that Mr. Star, a gentleman I often met at Mr. Lasserre's, should, as he himself informed L., first nail up a negro by the ears, then order him to be whipped in the severest manner, and then to have scalding water thrown over him, so that the poor creature could not stir for four months after. Another much-applauded punishment is drawing their slaves' teeth. One Colonel Lynch is universally known to have cut off a poor negro's legs, and to kill several of them every year by his barbarities.

It were endless to recount all the shocking instances of diabolical cruelty which these men (as they call themselves) daily practise upon their fellow creatures; and that on the most trivial occasions. I shall only mention one more, related to me by a Swiss gentleman, Mr. Zouberbuhler, an eye-witness, of Mr. Hill, a dancing-master in Charlestown. He whipped a she-slave so long, that she fell down at his feet for dead. When, by the help of a physician, she was so far recovered as to show signs of life, he repeated the whipping with equal rigour, and concluded with dropping hot sealing-wax upon her flesh. Her crime was overfilling a tea-cup.

These horrid cruelties are the less to be wondered at, because the government itself, in effect, countenances and allows them to kill their slaves, by the ridiculous penalty appointed for it, of about seven pounds sterling, half of which is usually saved by the criminal's informing against himself. This I can look upon as no other than a public act to indemnify murder.

Wednesday, August 11. Coming on board our ship, I found the honest captain had let my cabin to another. My flux and fever that has hung upon me forced me for some nights past to go into a bed; but now my only bed was a chest, on which I threw myself in my boots, and was not overmuch troubled with sleep till the morning. What was still worse, I then had no asylum to fly to from the captain; the most beastly man I ever saw a lewd, drunken, quarrelsome fool, praying, and yet swearing continually. The first sight I had of him was upon the cabin-floor, stark naked, and dead drunk.

Friday, August 13. The wind was still contrary; so that we were forced to lie off the bar, about five miles from Charlestown.

Monday, August 16. A faint breeze springing up, the pilot, weary of waiting a week to no purpose, said he would venture over the bar, though he feared there was not water enough. Accordingly we attempted it, and had got above half of the two miles between us and the sea, when a violent squall arose, and drove the ship before it with incredible swiftness. Before it began we were almost becalmed, so that it saved the ship, at least, from being aground, though with the immediate hazard both of that and our lives. The sailors were in great consternation, expecting to be stranded every moment. The pilot cursed the ship most heartily, and the hour he set foot in her. Having scraped along the ground for some minutes before, the ship at last stuck. She got clear, and stuck fast a second time; and immediately fell into seven-fathom water.

The mate afterwards told me it was one thousand to one but she had been lost by the captain's folly and ignorance, in letting fly the mainsail, while we struck on the bar; which was the surest way to fix her there, as it must have done had we not been on the very edge of it.

Tuesday, August 17. We were much surprised (the passengers, I mean) at finding, as soon as over the bar, that two of our twelve sailors were obliged to pump every half-hour.

Monday, August 23. I rose in the night to appease a quarrel between the second mate and the captain, who was continually interrupting the officers in their duty; giving out, as they informed me, such orders as would, if followed, cost them the ship and their lives. His indignation at present was occasioned by their furling some of the sails in the greatest squall we have yet met with.

Thursday, August 26. We saw a brigantine standing to the windward of us, but quickly lost sight of her. Had she come near us, Mr. Appee and I intended to have gone on board her; for we cannot yet believe we shall come to England in this ship.

Friday, August 27. We came to an allowance of water, the captain knowing nothing of what we had on board, till the officers informed him. Indeed, at his rate of drinking we must quickly come to a shorter allowance; for while any of his half-hogshead of rum remains, here will be nothing but punch, and drams, and drunkenness without end.

This morning Mr. Appee laid aside his mask. He began by telling me all Mr. Oglethorpe had ever said to him, particularly his inmost thoughts of my brother and me; that he ridiculed our pretended fasting in the ship; that he took all my abstemiousness for mere hypocrisy, and put on for fear of my brother, for he saw how very uneasy I was under the restraint; that he much blamed my carelessness, my closeness, my frightening the people, and stirring them up to mutiny, &c., &c.; that he found I apprehended being turned out of my office, and therefore pretended to be weary of it; that to save my reputation he had found me an errand to England, but never expected my return, any more than my brother's going to the Indians, which he well knew he never intended, but he would make his own use of him; that he greatly admired his *finesse* in offering to go to the Choctaws in all haste, but at the same time procuring the Germans to dissuade him. In a word, he believed him to have a little sincerity, but more vanity; me to have much vanity, but no sincerity at all.

I asked Appee whether his judgement was the same. He answered, 'Yes;' that my brother, he believed, was labouring to establish a character for sanctity; was exceedingly subtle, keeping me in the dark, as well as all others, yet credulous, and easy to be imposed upon himself; that he pitied his ignorance, in taking him (Appee) to be sincere; particularly in regard to his breaking off with Miss Bovey, which he intended, not in pursuance of his ghostly advice, but of Mr. Oglethorpe's, who had told him she was below his aspiring genius; that after his fine talk with my brother, he never made the least alteration in his own behaviour, or thought any farther about it.

While he was giving this blessed account of himself, I could not help reflecting on the profound sagacity and spiritual discernment of my brother and myself; particularly *his,* who was born for the benefit of knaves. *Si vult decipi, decipiatur.* For my own part, I will never imitate, I will ever beware of, men, as He who best knows them advises. I will not think all men rogues till I find them otherwise (according to Appee's avowed principle), but I will insist upon a far different probation from what my brother requires before I take any one into my confidence.

I next inquired what his thoughts were of me. He frankly replied, he took me to be partly in earnest; but I had a much greater mind to please myself than to please God. Yet as for money, I did not much value it; but in my eagerness for pleasure and praise I was a man after his own heart: that as I could not hold it, he wished I would leave oft my strictness, for I should then be much better company.

As for himself, he said his only principle was an insatiable thirst of glory; that Georgia was too narrow a sphere for him, and that therefore he should never see it more. Yet he desired my friendship, because I had learning, was sincere, and of his temper; but he should like me much better if I were not a parson. I had before let him into my own affairs, and read him my letter of resignation to Mr. Oglethorpe. His remark upon that was, 'It is finely calculated for the end you propose the engaging Mr. Oglethorpe's opinion and interest; but he will understand you.'

Saturday, August 28. After a restless, tempestuous night, I hardly rose at eight. Our happier captain, having got his dose, could sleep a day and a night upon the stretch, and defy either pumps or squall to wake him.

Monday, August 30. At noon we were alarmed by an outcry of the sailors, at their having continued pumping several hours without being able to keep the water under. They desired the captain to put into some port, before they were got out to sea too far for returning; but he was too drunk to regard them. At five the sailors came down in a body to the great cabin, waked and told him it was as much as their lives were worth to proceed on the voyage unless their leaks were stopped; that he remembered it was as much as ever they could do to keep the ship above water in their passage from Boston, being forced to pump without ceasing; that the turpentine fell down upon, and choked up, the pumps continually; nor was it possible to get at it, or to hold out in such continual labour; which made them so thirsty, they could not live on their allowance of water; that they must come to shorter still, through his neglect to take in five more hogsheads of water, as his mate advised him; that he owned they had no candles for half the voyage: on all which accounts they begged him to consider whether their common safety did not require them to put in at some land, for more water and candles, and, above all, to stop their leaks. The captain, having now slept out his rum, replied, To be sure, the men talked reason, and, without consulting any of his officers, immediately gave orders to stand away for Boston.

Saturday, September 4. Appee laid a train for the captain, and betrayed him into talking lewdly; for which I reproved him too sharply, and thereby increased his beastliness. He abused me plentifully, till I ceased to take any notice of him. In the evening he set upon me again; but I turned from him, and talked Latin to Zouberbuhler. This made him more outrageous. He blew out the candle by which I was writing. Zouberbuhler lit it; and he blew it out again: on which we all set upon him; I only talking Latin or Greek. He told me I was drunk, mad, an emissary, a Jesuit, a devil; but could not get one English word from me. The gentlemen, particularly Appee, baited him to his heart's content; and having laughed upon the stretch till near midnight, we then suffered the poor beast to return to his litter. The next day we said neither good nor bad to him; but he was not continent of speech. His indignation was mostly vented upon me, 'the arch-rebel,' as he called me, for my 'audacious talk.' In the evening he again put out Zouberbuhler's candle; upon which Appee pulled out the spicket of the rum, and let it run about the cabin. This was the cruellest punishment [that] could have been devised; and farther heightened by our mirth at his inimitable resentment. Zouberbuhler lighted up the candle in his own cabin every now and then, bringing it into the great cabin; and when the captain (whose motions were not of the nimblest) had come out of bed to put it out, Zouberbuhler carried it back again. He called down his men ten times, ordering them to bind us in our beds, to our and their no small diversion. He offered to get at the candle in Zouberbuhler's cabin; but the Swiss stood sentinel at his cabin-door, and then he might as well have wrenched a bone from Cerberus. The captain gave it over as impossible, drank a hearty dram, and dropped asleep.

Wednesday, September 15. This is the first time I have heard a sailor confess it was a storm. We lay under our mainsail, and let the ship drive, being by conjecture about sixty leagues from Boston, upon George's Bank; though, as we hoped, past the shoals in it. The captain never troubled himself about anything; but lay snoring even in such a night as the last, though frequently called, without ever stirring, either for squalls, or soundings, or shoals.

In the afternoon the mate came down, having sounded, and found forty, and soon after twenty, fathom; told the captain he apprehended coming into shoaler water still; and therefore it would be necessary to reef the foresail and mainsail in readiness, that in case we fell foul of the shoals (being upon George's Bank, and in a storm), the ship might have head-way, to get clear again. This the captain absolutely refused; and, though told it could do no possible harm, and might be the saving of the ship and us, persisted in his obstinacy; so that the mate left him to sleep, and the ship to take care of itself. But it pleased God to abate the storm, and on Thursday, about twelve, entirely to remove it.

Monday, September 20. At seven, Mr. Graham, the first mate, came to ask for directions, as he constantly does, and the captain as constantly shifting him off, and leaving the whole management of the ship to him, or chance, or anybody. The conversation being somewhat remarkable, I took it down in shorthand, as they were speaking it.

MATE. 'Captain Indivine, what would you have us do? What course would you have us to steer to-night?'

CAPTAIN. 'Even what course you will. We have a fair wind.'

M. 'Yes, sir; and it drives us full upon the land, which cannot be many leagues off.'

C. 'Then I think you had best keep forward.'

M. 'Would you have us go on all night, and venture running upon the land?'

C. 'I don't know. Go on.'

M. 'But there are shoals and rocks before us.'

C. 'Why, then, have a good look-out.'

M. 'But you cannot see twice the ship's length. What would you order me to do?'

C. 'These rebels and emissaries have excited you to come and ask for orders. I don't know what you mean.'

M. 'Sir, nobody has excited me. I come, as it is my duty, to my captain for directions.'

C. 'Have you a mind to quarrel with me?'

M. 'I have a mind to know what you will do.'

C. 'Nay, what will you do, if it come to that?'

M. 'Am I your captain? or you mine?'

C. 'I am your captain, and will make you know it, Mr. Man. Do what I order you; for you must and shall.'

M. 'Why, sir, you order me nothing.'

C. 'You would not have me come upon deck myself, sure.'

M. 'If you did, I should not think it would be much amiss. Some captains would not have stirred off deck a moment in such a night as this. Here you lie, without so much as ever once looking out, to see how things are.'

C. 'Yes, I have been upon deck this very day.'

M. 'But you have taken no account of any thing, or given yourself the least trouble about the ship, for many days past.

C. 'It is all one for that. I know where we are exactly.'

M. 'How far do you think we may be from land?'

C. 'Why, just thirty-five leagues. I am sure of it.'

M. 'How is that possible? You have taken no observation this fortnight; nor have we got one these four days.'

C. No matter for that. I know we are safe.'

M. 'The most skilful sailor alive cannot know it. Be pleased only to declare what you would have done. Shall we sail on? Shall we lay by? Shall we alter our course? Shall we stand in and off?' He went on repeating such questions again and again; but as to giving an answer, the captain chose to be excused; till the mate, quite out of patience, having waited an hour to no purpose, left him; and the captain concluded all with, 'Jack, give me a dram!'

Tuesday, September 21. The sailors, who were upon deck all night, saw three large ships coming, as they supposed, out of the bay; but in vain attempted to speak with them. At three I was waked by a cry of 'Land!' The mate said we were just upon it; for he saw the light of the watch-house; and if they did not tack about immediately, they would be upon the rocks, which lay just before them under the water. At the same time it blew a storm. The uproar was so great that it even waked the captain, who started up, ran to his rum, drank a hearty draught, and then looked upon deck; but not much liking things there, came down again immediately, cried, 'Aye, aye; all will be well'; and dropped asleep again.

Wednesday, September 22. Having sailed for some hours without discovering land, we began to think the light which the mate had seen was of some ship, and not the lighthouse. At two we made land; which the men soon found to be Cape Cod, about eighteen leagues from Boston. The wind blew from shore, yet we kept our course. At midnight the storm gave place to a calm. These have constantly succeeded each other since our leaving Charlestown.

Thursday, September 23. The fineness of the weather invited even Mr. Appee upon deck, who usually disposes of twenty-three of the twenty-four hours in bed. His vanity betrayed him into farther discoveries of himself. He laboured to show me the only difference between us lay in externals, through the difference of our education. I had the same views that he had, but was forced by the restraints of a narrower education to dissemble those inclinations which he had given a loose to. The case was the same with my brother: a much better hypocrite, he said, than me, and who would have made an excellent Jesuit. But Mr. Oglethorpe understood him, though for his own convenience he would not seem to do so.

Upon my asking him how he accounted for the great pains my brother had taken with him, he readily answered, That was all grimace. My brother could not but be mightily pleased with the reputation such a convert would gain to his sanctity, which had charms to win over so wild a young gentleman of his parts. 'But how could you bear him so long, if you had no esteem for him, or regard to his advice?' 'Why, it was so new a gratification to me to be thought religious, that I found no difficulty in keeping on the mask: and I had got such a knack of going to prayers and sacrament, that I don't know but I should have been actually caught at last.'

Friday, September 24. Being within sight of the light-house, at nine in the morning, the pilot came on board us. At two I gladly obeyed his hasty summons, and went into his boat with the other passengers, bidding an hearty farewell to our wretched ship, and more wretched captain, who for the last two days had, most happily for us, lain dead drunk on the floor, without sense or motion.

I was at leisure now to contemplate a prospect entirely new, and beautiful beyond all I had ever seen. We sailed smoothly on, in a vast basin, as it seemed, bounded on all sides with small innumerable islands. Some of these were entire rock, in height and colour not unlike Dover cliffs: others steep, and covered with woods. Here and there lay a round hill, entirely clothed with green; and all at such equal distances, that the passages seemed artificially made, to admit the narrow streams between.

Having passed one of these passages, we were presented with a new set of hills, and rocks, and woods, in endless variety; till we came to the castle, three miles from Boston. From thence we had a full view of the town, stretched out a mile and a half upon the shore, in a semicircle. We landed at Long Wharf, which we walked straight up, having a row of houses on one side, and near two hundred sail of ships on the other. I lodged in a public-house; went to bed at eleven. Appee followed me, drunk, between one and two in the morning.

Saturday, September 25. I called several times at Mr. Price, the Commissary's, before I found him at home. At first he looked as not believing me to be a clergyman (my ship-clothes not being the best credentials). But when I returned in my habit (Dr. Cutler having met him meantime, and informed him of me), he received me very cordially, and pressed me to live with him while I stayed in Boston.

Sunday, September 26. I preached in the morning at Dr. Cutler's church, in the afternoon at Mr. Price's, on the one thing needful.

In the evening I first fell into company with Mr. John Chicheley, a right honest zealous advocate for the Church of England, who has, on that account, been cruelly persecuted by the Presbyterians.

Thursday, September 30. In the morning I waited upon the Governor. At noon Mr. Millar, a good-natured clergyman, visited me. The rest of this and the following day I employed in writing to my friends at Charlestown.

Friday, October 1. I wrote to my brother concerning my return to Georgia, which I found myself inclined to refer wholly to God.

Saturday, October 2. I rode out with Mr. Price, in his chaise, to see the country, which is wonderfully delightful. The only passage out of town is a neck of land about two hundred yards over; all the rest being encircled with the sea. The temperate air, the clear rivulets, and the beautiful hills and dales, which we everywhere met with, seemed to present the very reverse of Georgia.

Sunday, October 3. After near two months want of it, I again enjoyed the benefit of the sacrament, which I assisted Dr. Cutler to administer. I preached on 'There the wicked cease from troubling, and there the weary are at rest': as I did again in the afternoon for Mr. Price, though I found my strength sensibly abated.

Monday, October 4. I rode with Mr. and Mrs. Price, Dr. Cutler, his son, and Mr. Brig (two Cambridge scholars), to see Mr. Millar, at Braintree. At our return we found Mr. Davenport, who was come to see me, a worthy clergyman, as deserving of the name as any I see in New England.

Tuesday, October 5. I dined at Mr. Plasted's, a London acquaintance of my brother's; who from thence took occasion to find me out, and showed me all the friendship and civility he could, while I stayed in Boston. After dinner I drove Mr. Cutler to Cambridge. I had only time to observe the civility of the Fellows, the regularity of the buildings, and pleasantness of the situation.

Saturday, October 9. I was dragged out to consult Dr. Graves about my increasing flux. He prescribed a vomit, from which I received much benefit.

Sunday, October 10. I recovered a little strength in the sacrament; but my body was extremely weakened by preaching twice.

Tuesday, October 12. I supped with several of the clergy, at Mr. Chicheley's, who entertained us very agreeably with his adventures. He seems to have excellent natural parts, much solid learning, and true primitive piety; is acquainted with the power, and therefore holds fast the form, of godliness; obstinate as was my father in good, and not to be borne down by evil.

Thursday, October 14. I was taken up with the clergy, in drawing up a recommendation of him to the Bishop of London, for orders. The Bishop had been formerly frightened from ordaining him, by the outcries of the Presbyterians. They were wise to keep a man out of the ministry who had in a private capacity approved himself such a champion for the Church.

Saturday, October 16. My illness increasing, notwithstanding all the doctors could do for me, I began seriously to consider my condition; and at my evening hour of retirement found benefit from Pascal's prayer in sickness.

Sunday, October 17. While I was talking at Mr. Chicheley's on spiritual religion, his wife observed that I seemed to have much the same way of thinking with Mr. Law. Glad I was and surprised to hear that good man mentioned; and confessed, all I knew of religion was through him. I found she was well acquainted with his *Serious Call;* and has one of the two that are in New England. I borrowed it, and passed the evening in reading it to the family (Mr. Williams's, where I have been some days). His daughter and he seemed satisfied and affected.

Monday, October 18. Many appointed days of embarkation had come and gone, without our embarking; but this was certainly to be the last. Accordingly Mr. Millar came very early to attend me to the ship. I took occasion to mention the book I had borrowed of his sister, Mrs. Chicheley, and read him the characters of Cognatus and Uranius. He liked them much, and promised he would carefully read the whole. Breakfast and dinner passed, but [there was] no summons to go on board.

Tuesday and Wednesday I grew worse and worse; and on Thursday, October 21, was forced to keep my chamber through pain. Appee came, and laboured all he could to dissuade me from the voyage, promising himself to deliver my letters and papers, and excuse me to Mr. Oglethorpe. Mr. Price, Williams, &c., joined him: but I put an end to their importunity by assuring them nothing less than death should hinder my embarking.

Friday, October 22. All things being at last in readiness, the wind providentially changed, and afforded me three days more to try experiments. Within that time I vomited, purged, bled, sweated, and took laudanum, which entirely drained me of the little strength I had left. It may be of use hereafter to remember Appee's behaviour at Boston. He gave out that his design in coming to Georgia had been to take charge of the people there: but finding Mr. Oglethorpe just such a genius as himself, he thought his own stay there was not so necessary, but he might safely quit the interest of the colony; which, had it not been to such a hand, he could never have prevailed upon himself to do: that at present he was unresolved where to bestow himself; only that it should be on that part of mankind which needed him the most: that he was going to England about matters of the last importance. Two or three letters of no moment, he said, I carried; but all secret dispatches, to the Duke of Newcastle, and other Ministers of State, he was charged with. From the court of Great Britain he was to be sent Envoy to Spain. His money, a few hundred pounds, he had (in some companies) sent before him to England; in others had turned it into silver, and freighted Indivine's ship.

Monday, October 25. I waked surprisingly better, though not yet able to walk. This morning Dr. Graves came over from Charlestown to see me, gave me physic and advice, which he likewise left in writing; but would take no fee for either. The same civility I received from Dr. Gibbons, Dr. Gardener, and others. A little after Mr. Chicheley came, and brought me a summons to go aboard. Mr. Price drove me to the wharf, having called by the way on some of my new friends, from whom I have received all the instances of kindness in their power to show.

When we came to the wharf, the boat was not ready; so we were forced to wait half an hour in the open cold air. Mr. Chicheley helped me into the boat, and covered me up. In about two hours we reached the ship; and with Mr. Zouberbuhler, Mr. Appee, Mr. Cutler, and Mr. Brig, went on board. I lay down in the state-room, less fatigued with the passage than I expected.

Finding Appee wanted his state-room again, I quitted it, and accepted Mr. Cutler's offer of his cabin. I had a tolerable night, though stripped of the conveniences I so long enjoyed on shore.

Tuesday, October 26. I entered upon the doctor's regimen, and quickly found the benefit.

When five leagues onward on our voyage, the wind changing forced us back again. In the evening it came fair, and by the next day carried us clear of all land.

Wednesday, October 27. I began public prayers in the great cabin. We had seldom any present but the passengers. I had not yet strength to read the lesson, nor attention for any harder study than Clarendon's *History*. In the night I was much disquieted by the colic.

Thursday, October 28. The captain warned me of a storm approaching. In the evening, at eight, it came, and rose higher and higher, after I thought it must have come to its strength; for I did not lose a moment of it, being obliged by the return of my flux to rise continually. At last the long-wished-for morning came, and brought no abatement of the storm. There was so prodigious a sea that it quickly washed away our sheep, and half our hogs, and drowned most of our fowl. The ship had been new caulked at Boston; how carefully, it now appeared: for being deeply laden, the sea streamed in at the sides so plentifully, that it was as much as four men could do, by continual pumping, to keep her above water. I rose and lay down by turns, but could remain in no posture long; strove vehemently to pray, but in vain; persisted in striving, yet still without effect. I prayed for power to pray, for faith in Jesus Christ, continually repeating His name, till I felt the virtue of it at last, and knew that I abode under the shadow of the Almighty.

It was now about three in the afternoon, and the storm at the height. I endeavoured to encourage poor Mr. Brig and Cutler, who were in the utmost agony of fear. I prayed with them, and for them, till four; at which time the ship made so much water, that the captain, finding it otherwise impossible to save her from sinking, cut down the mizen mast. In this dreadful moment, I bless God, I found the comfort of hope; and such joy in finding I could hope, as the world can neither give nor take away. I had that conviction of the power of God present with me, overruling my strongest passion, fear, and raising me above what I am by nature, as surpassed all rational evidence, and gave me a taste of the divine goodness.

At the same time I found myself constrained in spirit to bear witness to the truth, perhaps for the last time, before my poor friend Appee. I went to him, declared the difference between one that feareth God and one that feareth Him not; avowed my hope, not because I had attained, but because I had endeavoured it; and testified my expectation, if God should now require my soul of me, that He would receive it to His mercy.

My poor friend was convinced, but stupid; owned the happiness of the most imperfect Christian; an happiness he himself was a stranger to; and therefore, he said, all his refuge was, in time of danger, to persuade himself there was none. Mr. Cutler frequently calling upon God to have mercy upon his soul, Appee confessed he greatly envied him, as he had no manner of concern for his own. I advised him to pray. He answered, it was mocking God to begin praying in danger, when he had never done it in safety. I only added, I then hoped if God spared him now, he would immediately set himself about working out his salvation, which depended on the one condition of exchanging this world for the next. Mr. Zouberbuhler was present at this conference, and behaved as a Christian ought to do.

I returned to Mr. Brig and Mr. Cutler, and endeavoured from their fear to show them the want of religion, which was intended for our support on such occasions; urged them to resolve, if God saved them from this distress, that they would instantly and entirely give themselves up to Him.

The wind was still as high as ever, but the motion rather less violent since the cutting the mast; and we did not ship quite so much water. I laid me down, utterly exhausted; but my distemper was so increased, it would not suffer me to rest. Toward morning the sea heard and obeyed the divine voice, Peace, be still!

Sunday, October 31. My business to-day (may it be the business of all my days!) was to offer up the sacrifice of praise and thanksgiving. Then we all joined in thanks for our deliverance. Most of the day I was on the bed, faint, and full of pain. At night I rose to prayers, but could not read them. I took a vomit, which gave me immediate ease, in which I passed the rest of the night.

Monday, November 1. In the afternoon the wind rose, and promised a storm. I endeavoured to prepare myself and companions for it. It did not fail our expectation; but was not so violent as the last. The sea broke over us every ten minutes; and the ceaseless noise of the pumps either kept off sleep, or continually interrupted it.

Tuesday, November 2. Still the poor sailors could have no respite; and as their strength abated, their murmurings increased. At night, when almost exhausted, they were relieved by a calm.

Wednesday, November 3. In the evening the wind arose again, and with that the sea, which at ten broke in through one of the dark lights and filled the great cabin. It was vain to look for rest in such a hurricane. I waited till two in the morning for its abatement; but it continued all the following day in full majesty.

On *Friday, November* 5, we met a ship bound for Boston, which had been ten weeks on her passage from Bristol, and forced in the last storm to throw most of her cargo overboard. Being short of provisions, they desired a barrel of beef, which our captain very readily sent them (though at the expense of much time and pains), and a cag [keg] of rum, to encourage their sailors to pump.

The wind came fair about midnight, but soon returned to the same quarter.

Monday, November 8. My flux returned with great violence.

Tuesday, November 9. The men came down and declared they could keep the water under no longer, it gaining upon them every moment. Therefore they desired the captain would be pleased to lighten the ship. He told them he knew what he had to do; bade them return to their pumping, and ordered others to take in all the sails but the mainsail. He stayed some time (as he since told us, that he might not discourage *us*), and then went up; and as we lay by stopped several leaks upon deck. This did considerable service; though it was still the constant business of four men to keep the ship from filling.

During this time I often threw myself upon the bed, seeking rest, but finding none. I asked of God to spare me a little, that I might recover strength; then cast my eye upon the word: 'For My name's sake will I defer Mine anger; and for My praise will I refrain for thee, that I cut thee not off' (Isa. xlviii. 9). My soul immediately returned to its rest, and I no longer felt the continuance of the storm.

Wednesday, November 10. Towards night it pleased God to abate the wind, so that I once more enjoyed the comfort of sleep.

Saturday, November 13. Never was a calm more seasonable than that which Providence this day sent us. The men were so harassed, they could work no longer; and the leaks in creased so fast, that no less than their uninterrupted labour could have kept the vessel from foundering. All hands were now employed in stopping the leaks. The captain himself told us he had been heartily frightened yesterday with a danger he would now acquaint us with, since it was over: the total stoppage of one of the pumps. He further informed us that he had stopped several openings in the sides of the ship, wide enough to lay his fingers in; so that he wondered the poor men had been able to keep her above water; and added that the utmost he hoped for was that they might hold out till they could reach some of the western islands. Just as the men had finished their work, the calm gave place to a fair wind.

Tuesday, November 23. I imparted to Mr. Zouberbuhler my intention of discarding Appee as soon as we landed. He told me he wondered I had not done it before; for he was such a man, so unprofitable, so pernicious, that he himself would not be bound to go another voyage with him for all the world; that he was so excessively vain, he thought himself admired wherever he came; and I was so fond of him, that, for all my talk of parting, I could not live without him. He added, he was so notorious a liar that he had long since ceased to believe one word he said; and so utterly irreligious that it was impossible to make a friend of him. He talked so well on this subject that I was convinced he is not the mere man of honour Appee had represented him; but has some better principle than the dream of a shadow to depend upon.

At midnight I was waked by a great uproar. So prodigious a sea broke upon the ship, as filled it, and half-drowned the men upon deck; though by a particular providence none were washed overboard. The swell lasted something longer than the rain, and high wind; and in the morning we had our fair wind again; being the twelfth day since it was first commanded to attend us.

In the afternoon we had another short but fierce blast, which brought the wind still fairer for our running into the Channel, whence all agreed we could not be far distant. At night I found Mr. Zouberbuhler alone, who, anti cipating what I intended to say, addressed me very cordially, desiring my friendship and correspondence; complained of having been linked so long to Appee, that he was become dead like him, though he had had a fear of God, and some acquaintance with Him, till this fatal voyage. He was full of care and thought about his countrymen, whether he should bring them to New England or Georgia. In the latter, he said, he saw little encouragement for true piety (which many of his poor Swiss were yet possessed of), and feared if they were settled there they would be corrupted, like the miserable Purisburgers. He told me Appee had proffered, if his Spanish embassy failed, to attend him to Switzerland; but he would never more trust such a man near him, or his people: such an abominable liar, scoundrel, and thief; one who had been forced to fly his country and the pursuit of justice, for robbing his father of three hundred guineas.

A fair account of my friend Appee and of the twenty-four pounds I had lent him! That a Dutchman should cheat me is nothing strange: but how did he evade the wary eye of Mr. Oglethorpe? Happy Miss Bovey, to be delivered by death from such a man!

On Thursday night our wind failed us. When it was first sent, we had not, in three weeks' sailing, reached the banks of Newfoundland, which is a third part of our way: but this fort night has almost brought us home. The next day I was perfectly satisfied in the wind's turning against us.

Saturday, November 27. Towards the evening it came fair as we could wish.

Ecce iterum Crispinus! Mr. Zouberbuhler came to me, full of abhorrence. 'That Appee,' said he, 'is a very devil, made up of falseness and lies! He is ever railing against you, behind your back, to the captain and passengers, ridiculing the prayers, &c. He tells the captain (as he did everybody at Boston), that you are so ignorant, Mr. Oglethorpe was forced to send him to take care of you. At Charlestown he declared, in all companies, he was come with full powers to put an end to the dispute between them and Georgia. Last night I overheard him giving a blessed account of you to Mr. Brig. As soon as ever I come to land I shall cast him off, and advise you to do the same: for while you suffer him near you, he will not fail to do you all the mischief he can.'

Monday, November 29. We were waked be tween six and seven by the captain crying out, Land! It was the Lizard Point, about a league distant. What wind there was, it was for us. I felt thankful for the divine mercies.

While I was walking upon deck, Appee came up to me, *metuens tale votum ereptum a faucibus;* began with many professions of friendship, hoped all little misunderstandings would be forgot; fell into familiar discourse, as formerly; was sure I should never return to Georgia; where Mr. Oglethorpe would allow none but his creatures, or such as were some way subservient to his glory: 'which, take my word for it,' said he, 'is the principle of all his actions, as well as mine. Christianity he has about as much as myself. I have given him some unanswerable reasons against it.' He was undetermined where to spend the next year, but resolved to spend it all in quest of pleasure and glory and confident I was just of his mind.

Wednesday, December 1. The first thing I heard at daybreak was the captain in an outrageous passion; for the ship, which, according to the course he had ordered, ought to have been near the coast of France, was, through the carelessness of the mate, just upon the land at Shoreham. He told me that had not the day broke out as it did, the ship must have run aground; and then all the art of man could not have saved her; for we were land-locked on three sides, and had the wind right astern: so that it was with the utmost difficulty, and not till the afternoon, that we got clear. This lost us a day; for by the evening we should have reached the Downs.

Appee took me aside once more, to try his skill upon me; besought me not to alter my behaviour toward him when we should come to land; denied, as ever he hoped for salvation, that he had ever spoke or wrote disrespectfully of me; detested the thought of such treachery, with so many horrid imprecations, as I believed even a Dutchman would have trembled at. The burden of all was, John Bull and Nicholas Frog were too dear friends ever to think of parting. But John Bull begged to be excused. Though I stood in admiration of his parts, I did not choose they should be any longer exercised on me. In vain did he resume our lodging together. I was deaf on that ear, and shifted the discourse, which he still brought back again. 'Well, my dear friend, wherever you are,' said he, 'I will take a lodging next door.'

Thursday, December 2. By four in the after noon we came within sight of Beachy Head; but the wind freshening, by nine we found our selves almost unawares over against Dover. We fired a gun for a pilot, but none would come to us. We fell down into the Downs, over against Deal, and fired two more. The captain gave us warning that he expected a pilot in an hour or two, at the farthest. I returned thanks to God for bringing us to the haven where we would be; got my few things in readiness, and laid me down, without disquiet or impatience, for two or three hours.

Friday, December 3. At six the pilot came on board. It was with much difficulty we got down into his boat. The sea was so rough that nothing less than our late series of deliverances could have supported our confidence. In half an hour we reached the shore. I knelt down, and blessed the Hand that had conducted me through such inextricable mazes; and de sired I might give up my country again to God when He should require.

Zouberbuhler appeared full of gratitude to God, and affection to me. We all adjourned to an inn. Zouberbuhler and I walked to bespeak a coach. I joined with the passengers in an hearty thanksgiving for our safe arrival.

Between ten and eleven we set out in the coach; and by three reached Canterbury, and by ten Sittingbourne. I had intended to lie with Zouberbuhler; but upon an intimation from him, went and lay with Appee, to hinder his having a different kind of bedfellow.

Saturday, December 4. Appee was so very grievous to us that not only I, but all the passengers, resolved this should be the last day of their acquaintance. At six in the evening we came safe to London. I immediately took coach for Charles Rivington's, leaving my friend Appee, who promised to come next day and pay me what he owed me.

My namesake was much rejoiced to see me, and gave me great cause of rejoicing by his account of our Oxford friends.

Sunday, December 5. I received comfort with the sacrament at St. Paul's; and from thence went to Mr. Towers, who received me with great affection; and heartily congratulated me on my arrival, which my friends had long despaired of. He told me the agreeable news of Mr. Oglethorpe's being expected daily.

The next I waited upon was good old Sir John Philips, who received me as one alive from the dead. Here I heard a most blessed account of our friends at Oxford; their increase, both in zeal and number. I then hastened to Mr. Vernon, to deliver my letters. He received me very affectionately, and pressed me to live with him during my stay in London.

While we were talking, young Hutton called, having traced me thither, in order to carry me home with him. We took coach for my good old friend and host, his father. I entered with fear and trembling. My reception was such as I expected from a family that entirely loved me, but had given me over for dead, and bewailed me as their own child. A captain had told them that fifty per cent, assurance had been refused for Indivine's ship; and a report was spread abroad that she had been seen sink to the bottom. The motion of the stage and hackney coaches occasioned the return of my flux, which prevents me preaching or talking to my admirers. Many such I have gained by Mr. Ingham's magnificent Journal. My brother's Journal, too (the last I hope will ever be sent hither), is in every one's hands.

> *Libeat modo vivere, fient,*
> *Fient ista palam, cupient et in acta referri.*

Monday, December 6. I spent an hour at my uncle's, equally welcome and unexpected. They informed me my brother Hall was gone to a curacy, very melancholy, and impatient at the mention of Georgia; and that my sister Kezzy was gone to live with him.

> *Serpentes avibus geminentur, tigribus agnae.*

I waited upon Mr. Hutchinson, who soon fell upon the controverted points. Here also I had an invitation to make his house my home.

Tuesday, December 7. I called in the morning on Charles Rivington, who gave me letters and a Journal from my brother in Georgia. After leaving my secretary's book with Mr. Towers, I waited upon the Bishop of London. In the ante-chamber I began his Journal, and read it through without either surprise or impatience. His dropping my fatal letter I hope will convince him of what I never could his own great carelessness; and the sufferings *that* brought upon him, of his inimitable blindness. His simplicity in telling what and who were meant by the two Greek words (See John Wesley's *Journal,* Standard ed., Vol. I p. 260.) was 'outdoing his own outdoings.' Surely all this will be sufficient to teach him a little of the wisdom of the serpent, of which he seems as utterly void as his dear friend Mrs. H. is of the innocency of the dove.

In the midst of these reflections I was called in to deliver my letters. His Lordship desired me to come next morning, having much to say to me. I drove to Colonel Bladen, who was from home; then to Mrs. Pendarvis, where we passed an agreeable hour, in mutual accounts of our friends in England and America.

I returned to Mr. Hutton, where Dr. Hales, one of our Trustees, came to see me. Much discourse we had of Georgia, particularly of Miss Bovey's death, and my brother's persecutions among that stiff-necked people. He seems a truly pious, humble Christian, full of zeal for God, and love to man.

Wednesday, December 8. I waited on Colonel Bladen; and then on the Bishop, who asked abundance of curious questions, not worth remembering.

In the evening I obeyed a summons from my Lord Egmont, and gave him, as I did all I came to the speech of, a true account of the case between Georgia and Carolina.

Thursday, December 9. I called on Mr. Towers, who desired me by all means to go home, and keep there, whoever sent for me; promising, if he had any business, he would come to me. I took his advice, and kept my chamber some days, which, with Dr. Cockburn's electuary, almost perfectly recovered me.

Saturday, December 11. Mr. Brig and Cutler called, and informed me Captain Corney was heartily frightened by hearing on all sides Appee's real character; that he gave over for lost the money he had lent him, as well as that for passage and provisions.

Contrary to my doctor's advice, I ventured out Sunday, December 12, to the sacrament in Duke Street. Mrs. Rhodes challenged me after the service with, I am glad to see you. I hope you go back again to Georgia.

In the evening a multitude came, and went; most to inquire of their friends or relations in Georgia. I sent them away advocates for the colony.

Wednesday, December 15. About noon I waited upon the Trustees, at the office. It put me past all patience to hear they were reading Mr. Ingham's and my brother's Journals. I was called in, and delivered my letters for the Trustees. Lord Carpenter, being in the chair, desired me to speak that all the gentlemen might hear me. Mr. Towers interposed, and told them I was so weakened by my illness, that I could not speak aloud; and desired me to deliver my papers one by one, to be read by Mr. Virelst. At dinner they fell into discourse about the Missioners, whom as yet they mightily commend, and wish for more of them; as that their Journals might be forthwith printed, that the world might receive the benefit of their labours.

Thursday, December 16. I was extremely sick in the night, and by morning my flux returned.

Saturday, December 18. I began my twenty-seventh year in a murmuring, discontented spirit; reading over and over the third of Job.

Tuesday, December 21. I dined at my uncle's, (Mr. Matthew Wesley, who brought up Mrs. Hall.) who bestowed abundance of wit on my brother and his apostolical project. He told me, the French, if they had any remarkably dull fellow among them, sent him to convert the Indians. I checked his eloquence by those lines of my brother:

> To distant realms th' Apostle need not roam,
> Darkness, alas! and heathens are at home.

He made no reply; and I heard no more of my brother's apostleship.

Wednesday, December 22. I received a letter from Mr. Whitefield, offering himself to go to Georgia.

Thursday, December 23. I had a long conference with Lord Fitz waiter concerning Georgia. In the afternoon my old captain's owners came to desire me to testify the treatment I had received, for which reason I would not proceed [to England] with Indivine. This I promised with Zouberbuhler, if there should be occasion.

Sunday, December 26. I called upon my doctor, and was well chid for so doing. He told me that if I had not had a constitution of iron, I could not have held out so long; that he could do nothing for me, unless I would keep my chamber; through want of which I had undone all he had been doing, and had all to begin anew.

Wednesday, December 29. I called on Zouberbuhler, who gave me the poor Purisburgers case to read; an eternal monument of Carolina's infamous breach of faith. Soon after Mr. Lynn, his landlord, came in, and entertained us with some of Mr. Appee's adventures; who, when he came from Surinam, where he had gamed away a plantation his father gave him, was reduced to the last extremity, and taken in naked and starving, by one Mrs. Legg, who was quickly forced to turn him out again, for offering violence to a lady in her family.

> *Cedite Germani latrones, cedite Galli.*

He has not studied Gil Bias for nothing (his inseparable companion throughout our voyage). As to his boasts, a specimen Mr. Lynn helped me to may serve for all. 'I wish that dear man, Mr. Oglethorpe, would return. I am impatient to see him; but he is even with me. How would he throw open his arms to embrace me! We were always like two brothers. He could never be without me. We were constant bedfellows. Many an expedition have we made together; though, in faith, I had work enough of it as his secretary. What belonged to one, belonged to the other. He took a fancy to a gold watch of mine. I gave it him that instant. It cost me indeed twenty guineas; but that is a trifle between friends.'

Thursday, December 30. I waited upon the Bishop of London for some papers I had left with him, concerning the state of the colony. Some effect they seemed to have had; for he appeared less reserved than I have ever seen him. I took the opportunity to recommend Mr. Chicheley for orders; and he said, He should give in his name to the Society, in the list of missionaries.

1737

Monday, January 3. In the evening Mr. Zouberbuhler brought Captain Corney to see me; from whom I received the following narration:

I was walking with an officer last night, when, in the Strand, I met Mr. Appee, the gentleman I had been two days in quest of. I let him pass, to try if he would take any notice of me; but finding he would not, I called after him. He turned, ran to me, and embraced me with -

'**APPEE.** "Dear Captain Corney, I am over joyed to see you. It is my great misfortune that I could not do it sooner; but I have been so extremely ill, and have such a multitude of business upon my hands, and of such consequence, as made it impossible."

'**CAPTAIN.** "I did hope indeed to have seen you in these three weeks."

'**A.** "But, dear sir, you cannot conceive the load I have had upon me! What endless business of this Georgia! and all at this end of the town."

'**C.** "Well, since I have had the good fortune to meet you at last, we must take a glass of wine together."

'**A.** "That would be to me the greatest pleasure in life; but I am going home in all haste to dress, being forced abroad by business of the last importance."

'**C.** "Nay, but you shall bestow one half-hour upon me and my friend, since we have had the happiness of meeting you."'

With much ado he got him into the next tavern, and after some indifferent questions mentioned his promise to freight the ship, which is now clear, said he, and ready for the Georgia passengers.

'**A.** "That is the very thing I wanted to talk with you about. I look for Mr. Oglethorpe every hour; and as soon as ever he arrives, the business shall be done. You may depend upon it; for I can do anything with him."

'**C.** "Sir, I am infinitely obliged to you; but in the meanwhile I must pay off my men, and re-fit my ship, which you know has suffered much in the passage. This will stand me in a good deal of money; and therefore I should be glad to settle that small account betwixt us."'

'**A.** "It was the very thing I was just going to mention though it grieves me too. Surely I am the most unfortunate man breathing! Such disappointments and losses on all hands since my arrival! my father's failing! my mother's death! my dear friend Mr. Oglethorpe's delay! that really I am afraid it will be some days before I pay you."

The captain tried some time if he could not recover his money; but finding nothing was to be got by fair means, at last told the officer that was the man; and bade him do his duty. Appee started up and cried, 'I hope, captain, you are not in earnest! He is not really an officer!' 'Hands spake for Casca'; and the catchpole told him he was his prisoner, offering to read him his writ. Appee declined it, telling him he understood those things; and immediately fell to his entreaties; told the captain what an esteem he had for him; how he had everywhere extolled his honour, his good-nature, and generosity: conjured him by their past friendship to release him directly, 'otherwise,' says he, 'Mr. Wesley will hear of it, and bring his action for *his* money, which, with your debt, is all I owe in the world.'

The captain replied he had no intention to hurt him, but only to get his own money a mere trifle for Mr. Oglethorpe's secretary to pay! or, to be sure, his father would lay it down for him the moment he heard of his confinement.

'**A.** "I assure you, captain, if one shilling would set me free, I have not a relation in the world that would advance it for me."

'**C.** "Why, then, I find you have behaved yourself as scurvily toward them as you have toward me. In the ship you was an agent, a secretary, a statesman; but on shore I perceive you are a bite, and a scoundrel; and as such I will use you."

'**A.** "For God's sake, dear captain, have pity upon me. I will give you all I have; five pounds in money, my clothes, watch, buckles, sword, snuff-box, and hat.

'**C.** "Sir, I scorn to take a gentleman's clothes; for such you passed upon me: and had you sent me a single line, with, *Here are three or four guineas for you, Corney, and I will pay the rest when I am able,* I would never have given you or myself any farther trouble about it. But your design, from the beginning, was to cheat me; and I shall therefore make an example of you. In Boston, when I would have had you lay in less wine, you told me, What signified forty pounds New England money? Truly not much to you, who intended me to pay it. But how could you be so base, when I had laid in your provisions, and lent you money, to rob me of the three pounds for the letters?" His answer to the last indictment was plainly,

'**A.** "Necessity has no law."

'**C.** "None but an experienced rogue could have made such an answer. You thought me a soft, silly fellow, and was therefore resolved to skin me: but now you shall answer for all.'

'**A.** "Have patience with me till Mr. Oglethorpe comes; you shall then have your freight of passengers and money both. You may be sure of it; for I can have of him what money I please."

'**C.** "I do not believe a word of it. Did Mr. Oglethorpe see you in a jail, he would leave you there to condign punishment."

'**A.** "Oh, how can you think so, when I have so often told you how intimate we are, and on what important affairs he sent me to England? It is not my liberty I value; for that he will restore me to, the moment he hears of my confinement; but I fear I shall lose his good opinion."

'**C.** "I do not believe you ever had it; or that he sent you hither for any other reason, but to get rid of a vagrant, that would else corrupt his colony. If you can pay me my money, do; or I must leave you to justice.

'**A.** "Take my clothes in part of payment. I will give you my note for the remainder of the debt."

'**C.** "Would you give me your note for the whole twenty-two pounds, I would sell it the first man that would give me sixpence for it."

The captain continuing inexorable, Appee cried like a child: upon which he asked him how he could behave so abjectly, who had scorned on board to own himself in any danger (as soon as it was past), 'when I myself,' said he, 'had little hopes of our escaping?'

'**A.** "Oh, sir, imprisonment, or death itself, is nothing to me; but the loss of so dear a friend as Mr. Oglethorpe! this is what sits so heavy at my heart. But I hope you will not be so cruel as to rob me of him."

'**C.** "I shall be so just to myself, and the world, as to expose a common cheat, who lives upon the public, and lays all honest men, that do not know him, under contribution."

Saturday following the captain was prevailed upon by a friend of Appee (now in Newgate) to go hear if he had anything farther to propose. He began very oratorically; could not blame the captain for what he had done, but forgave him from his heart, and had still the utmost esteem and affection for him: always said, 'Captain Corney was a good-natured man, and a gentle man'; was sure, therefore, he would not ruin a poor young fellow, who was rising in the world, and on the very point of making his fortune. He then began casting up the worth of his snuff box, &c. His sword he valued at seven pounds, his bureau at four.

'**C.** "That bureau, Mr. Wesley told me, was a lady's in London."

'**A.** "Why, that is very true. I had really forgot it. However, a guinea I may ask her for the freight."

'**C.** "Sir, you talk like what you are. I expected when you sent for me, your father had supplied you with money to pay me."

'**A.** "I assure you once more, was I now going to be hanged, my father would not give a single shilling to save me from the gallows."

'**C.** "You give a fine account of yourself, and perfectly consistent with that you gave at Boston. Is it fit that such an one as you should be suffered any longer to impose upon honest people? It is well you are at the end of your rogueries."

'**A.** "I had a suspicion that you had laid a trap for me at Zouberbuhler's; but I was too wise to be caught there."

'**C.** "It is full as well that I have caught you here. You have been so ungrateful a scoundrel to me, that I was resolved to spend a little more money upon you."

'**A.** "I deserve it for a blockhead as I am, for not putting myself, as I intended, under the court of the green cloth."

'**C.** "Why, what a precious rogue you describe yourself! Can you, after this, expect any favour from me?"

'**A.** "I hope you will not take it ill, if I take the benefit of the Act, through which I can come out next term."

'**C.** "Oh, not at all, sir. Take the benefit of the Act, by all means. I would do so myself, was I in your place. But when you are ready to come out, I will give you your keeping there for one half-year longer."

Here Appee's friend, Mr. Joy, told him: 'You have used the captain so villainously that I am ashamed to have had any dealings with you. I cannot say one word against his resolution; and desire you would never send or write to me again, or to any of your friends; for we wash our hands of you, and from this hour shall think of you no more.'

With this speech he left him, and, walking with the captain, observed what a poor unhappy young fellow he was. 'That shipwreck of his, in particular, was as unfortunate an accident as one shall hear of.' 'What shipwreck?' says the captain. 'Why, in his passage from Carolina. Have you not heard of it?' 'No,' replied he, 'nor anybody else.' 'He told me,' says Joy, 'that the ship ran upon the rocks, and all the men were lost, but the boatswain, a boy, and himself; that as he clung upon a rock, a sea came and washed him off, dashing him upon another rock, with such violence that it broke his skull, a tooth, and three of his ribs, so that it cost him no less than ten guineas to the surgeon.'

This account I made the captain repeat two or three times, and took it down from him in shorthand. I asked what gave him the first suspicion of Appee's knavery. He answered that when the searchers had opened his bureau he saw several letters Appee had broken open, and a memorandum of nine hundred pounds currency he had taken up at Charlestown, upon (as he suspected) a forged bill of exchange.

Friday, January 7. The news was brought of Mr. Oglethorpe's arrival. The next day I waited on him, and received a relation of his wonderful deliverance in the Bristol Channel. The people of Carolina, he told me, were quite mad, had hired men to murder the Indians, the Spaniards, had burned Augusta, &c. He then inquired about Appee. I gave him some little account of his misbehaviour, together with an extract of my Journal. He seemed sorry he had ever employed him; talked admirably of resignation, and the impossibility of dying when it is not best.

Sunday, January 9. I saw him again with Mr. Towers. He told me he had read my Journal, which was writ with a great deal of spirit. I replied all I could answer for was that it was writ with a great deal of truth.

Thursday, January 13. I met Mr. Gershom at Mr. Oglethorpe's. He told me of Appee's cheating D__, a poor drunken P__, of his gold watch. Mr. Oglethorpe acquainted me that he had been sent to again by Appee, in Newgate. Upon my expressing pity for him, he added: 'I can do nothing. He has tied my hands. If I released him, it would confirm all his lies. We are such dear friends that I must even leave him where he is.'

Wednesday, January 19. Count Zinzendorf, just arrived from Germany, sent for me. When I came, he saluted me with all possible affection, and made me promise to call every day. From him I went to the Bishop of Oxford, where I met with an equally kind reception. He desired me to come as often as I could, without farther ceremony or invitation.

We had much talk of the state of religion, and of Count Zinzendorf's intended visit. Their bishops he acknowledged to have the true succession.

Thursday, January 20. I wrote and delivered my own state in a letter to the Count. He sent me to Mr. Oglethorpe, who talked much of the mischief of private journals, all which ought to be published, or never sent. A letter from my brother he read; and argued, I could not but think the writer much too free, too bold, too credulous.

Saturday, January 22. I called upon Mrs. Pendarvis, while she was reading a letter of my being dead. Happy for me had the news been true! What a world of misery would it save me!

In the afternoon I was overjoyed to meet at Mrs. Essen's my old friend Miss Granville.

Sunday, January 23. I met Bishop Nitschman at the Count's, and was introduced to the Countess: a woman of great seriousness and sweetness. I was present at their public service, and thought myself in a quire of angels.

Tuesday, January 25. I paid a visit to Dr. Hales, [1] in the country.

Wednesday, January 26. We took a walk to see Mr. Pope's house and gardens, justly called a burlesque upon human greatness. I was sensibly affected with the plain Latin sentence upon the obelisk in memory of his mother: *Ah, Editha! matrum optima, mulierum amantissima, vale!* How far superior to the most laboured elegy that he, or Prior himself, could have composed!

Sunday, January 30. At St. Martin's I heard an excellent sermon by Dr. Trapp, on, In your patience possess ye (or be ye master of) your souls; proving the miserable slavery of the passions.

Tuesday, February 1. I was again with the Bishop of Oxford, and told him the Bishop of London had declined having anything to do with Georgia, and said it belonged to the Archbishop only to unite the Moravians with us. He replied it was the Bishop of London's proper office; but bade me assure the Count we should acknowledge the Moravians as our brethren, and one Church with our own.

Wednesday, February 2. Mr. Oglethorpe told me, Appee, released from prison, desired to meet me at his house. The next morning I waited there some hours, to confront him; but no Appee appeared.

At nine I was with the Count, who seemed resolved to carry his people from Georgia, if they might not be permitted to preach to the Indians. He much pressed me to go with him to Germany; which I am very willing to do, if I can get clear of the Trustees.

Sunday, February 6. I had much conversation with the Count. Some of his words were, The Christian cannot yield to sin; cannot long fight against it; but must conquer it, if he will. Speaking of his own case, he said, he and a lady were in love with each other; till, finding something of nature, he resolved to renounce her; which he did, and persuaded her to accept of his friend. 'From that moment,' said he, 'I was freed from all self -seeking; so that for ten years past I have not done my own will in any thing, great or small. My own will is hell to me. I can just now renounce my dearest friend, without the least reluctance, if God require it.' He kissed and blessed me at parting.

Monday, February 7. Before I set out for Oxford I called upon the Count, and desired his prayers. He commended himself to our friends there; and promised, if any of them would write him, or the Brethren, they would answer them.

Tuesday, February 8. I came to Oxford, and took up my lodgings with Mr. Sarney. In the evening I met and encouraged our friends by the Count's and the Moravians example. Mr. Kinchin I found changed into a courageous soldier of Christ. I read them my brother's Journal.

Wednesday, February 9. I met and accompanied my friend Home to the Convocation, where we carried the election (I came down about) for Mr. Bromley, our old member three hundred and thirty-nine against one hundred and twenty-six.

I visited my old friends at the castle, and found honest Thomas Waite still a prisoner there. Mrs. Topping was gone where the prisoners rest together, and hear not the voice of the oppressor. Returning, I called at the Blue Posts, and found my old pupil, Robert Kirkham. We spent the evening, as before, in mutual exhortation.

Thursday, February 10. I talked with some of my old proselytes in College; paid my respects to the Dean, and met with a sharp expostulation for voting against him (as he called it). In an hour we came to a right understanding, and parted friends.

I dined with Mr. Woods, of Abingdon: the same kind, friendly man he was. In the evening I saw Mr. Carter and Banny Kirkham, and laboured to awaken one and confirm the other. At Mr. Sarney's I found good Mr. Gambold and Kinchin.

Friday, February 11. I exhorted poor languid Smith, and then Carter, to resume all their rules of holy living. In the afternoon I was with the Rector of Lincoln, who received me very affectionately.

Saturday, February 12. By nine at night I got back to the Count in London, and consulted him about my journey to Germany.

Tuesday, February 15. I told Mr. Oglethorpe of my desire of returning with him to Georgia, if I could be of any use there as a clergyman; but as to my secretary's place, I begged him to tell me where, when, and how I should resign it. He bade me think what I did; and when I had well considered the matter, he would talk with me farther.

Friday, February 18. In walking to St. Martin's I met my dearest friend Appee, who accosted me with inimitable assurance, and asked where he might meet me. I appointed Mr. Oglethorpe's, the next morning.

Saturday, February 19. I waited on Mr. Oglethorpe, with no great expectation of Appee. He was too wary to keep his appointment.

Sunday, February 20. Being to set out the next day for Tiverton, I went to take my leave of the Count, who invited me again to Germany, bade me not despair, and dismissed me with his blessing. My last words were, *Sit pax vobiscum:* to which he replied, *Et cum spiritu tuo.*

Monday, February 21. I came in the coach to Reading; and the next evening to Marlborough, where I found horses my brother Hall had sent to bring me to Wootton. With him and my sisters, Patt and Kez, I stayed till –

Monday, February 28, and then took horse for Bath; the next day I got to Wellington; and,

Wednesday, March 2, in the morning reached Tiverton. I ran upstairs to my sister, who received me with tears of joy. I saw Phill next, and last my brother, who seemed at least as well as when he left me at London, three years before. I went to comfort my mother, indisposed in her chamber.

Tuesday, March 8. I took horse, and on Thursday afternoon got back again to Wootton.

Tuesday, March 15. I set out for London in the Marlborough coach, which had been robbed morning and evening, for four days before. This fifth morning we passed unmolested. Scarce was I got to town, when they fell to robbing again.

Thursday, March 17. At Mrs. Pendarvis's I found Miss Granville and her brother, who pressed me to bear him company to Mickleton.

Tuesday, March 22. I set out at three in the Oxford coach with Mr. Granville and his sister, & Mr. Dews. (Anne Granville married Mr. John Dewes in 1740.)

Wednesday, March 23. I was much moved at hearing Mr. Gambold's history of my brother.

Thursday, March 24. Our company set out again for Mickleton, which we reached by night. We passed the time agreeably enough in walking, conversing, and reading.

Wednesday, March 30. I rode over to Stanton, where they were all overjoyed to see me; especially my first of friends, Varanes. (Miss Betty Kirkham.)

Wednesday, April 6. I had some conversation with Miss Granville about the fewness of those that are saved. How little is she advanced in the school of Christ, who is not convinced of this truth!

Saturday, April 9. In the evening I had the satisfaction of seeing Mr. Granville much affected with a chapter he had been reading of Mr. Law. He desired his sister might hear it. I read it a second time, and took that opportunity of pressing upon him a daily retirement.

Thursday, April 28. I took horse with Mr. Granville and Dews. The former left us at Compton, and we rode on towards Spilsbury.

Saturday, April 30. I got back to Mr. Sarney's, weary and faint, and in a fever, through want of sleep.

Monday, May 2. Between one and two in the morning I betook myself to my usual bed, the floor. Charles Graves breakfasted with me, and owned with tears he had never felt any true joy but in religion. I earnestly recommended Law to him.

At noon I visited Mr. Gambold, right glad to see me. I found him much cheerfuller than usual: his sister just the same. In the after noon I talked with the prisoners, very attentive; with the Dean, very kind and friendly.

Tuesday, May 3. At two Mr. Sarney rose to pray for me. I rose too, and set out for London, which I reached in a few hours.

Thursday, May 5. I met Virelst and counsel at Mr. Oglethorpe's, about the hearing they are shortly to have before the Board of Trade. When they were gone, Mr. Oglethorpe said if the Government had dropped Georgia, he would not let the poor people perish, but sell his estate, which he could do for £45,000, and support them upon the interest.

Friday, May 20. At her desire, I waited upon Lady Betty Hastings. Her inquiries about Georgia were interrupted by the Bishop of Gloucester's coming.

Saturday, May 21. I rode out of town to meet my brother and sister from Tiverton, and attended them to Mr. Powel's.

Monday, May 30. I carried my brother to the good Archbishop, who received us very kindly.

Wednesday, June 1. I accepted an invitation from Mrs. Benson, and rode down to Cheshunt Nunnery. Miss Kitty and Mrs. Johnson were there before me. I was much delighted both with the place and company. After dinner I missed my letter-book, and rode back to town, seeking it in vain. By seven next morning I was at the Nunnery again, and returned to London in the afternoon.

Friday, June 3. Between six and seven this evening I took horse for Cheshunt, eighteen miles from London; got there by nine; and the next morning rode eighteen miles farther, to Hatfield, to see my sister Nancy. In the after noon I returned to the Nunnery.

Trinity Sunday, June 5. We all went in an hired coach to Warmley; where I preached Few saved, and was pleased to see the family stay the unexpected sacrament. In the evening I rode back to town.

Monday, June 6. At ten we were again before the Board of Trade. Till twelve Carolina side was heard. Then our counsel (confused enough) was heard for Georgia.

Wednesday, June 8. I made affidavit in Chan cery Lane, as to what I knew relating to Georgia. At one I called upon my uncle, and found him exceeding ill.

Thursday, June 9. At the Board, part of our Charter and Acts were read, &c. I declared upon oath that all the traders licensed were supposed to be within Georgia. After my affidavit was read, Murray made our defence; but so little to Mr. Oglethorpe's satisfaction, that he started up, and ran out. I dined with my brother at Lord Oxford's. (Note: The second Earl, friend of Pope and Swift.) Lady Oxford, Lord Duplin, and the famed Lady Mary were of the company.

Saturday, June 11. I found my uncle dying. He pressed my hand, showed much natural affection, and bade me give his love to his sister. I spent the evening at Cheshunt, in reading Mr. Law to the family my usual employment there.

Sunday evening. I heard that my uncle died a little after I left him.

Monday, June 13. I waited on my brother and sister a little way on their road to Tiverton.

On Wednesday I breakfasted at the Nunnery.

On Thursday night I attended my uncle to his grave.

Friday, June 17. I heard the last of my friend Appee's adventures here, from one Mr. Laba, a cutler; from whom he had just stole a watch, and run away with it to Paris.

Saturday, June 18. I was before the Board of Trade for the last time, to hear Carolina's reply to Georgia. I spent the rest of the month between Cheshunt and Hatfield.

Saturday, July 2. I was at the Nunnery; and the next day preached at Hatfield. I slept at Cheshunt.

Monday, July 4. In the evening I set out for Oxford. I came thither the next day, where James Hutton had got before me. In the evening young Graves came to me at Sarney's, in an excellent temper. I encouraged him to go on in the narrow way; and strongly recommended stated hours of retirement.

Thursday, July 7. I pressed the same upon poor Smith, in our walk to Mr. Gambold's, where I found my sister Kezzy. I got back to dinner with Lady Cox and her sisters. In the evening Graves told me that on this day he first felt the beginnings of the change; and was convinced of the reality of what he only believed before upon my brother's and my testimony. He appeared full of joy and love.

Saturday, July 9. I set out with James, for Wootton. Quite spent, I laid me down, and slept for a quarter of an hour upon the ground. By two we reached Maryborough, and by four, Wootton. My mother was lately come thither from Tiverton.

Monday, July 11. Meeting Ch. [Graves] at Bath, we could get no farther. He carried us to see the quarries; where I narrowly missed being dashed to pieces. On Wednesday, July 13, we came safe to Tiverton.

Saturday, July 23, and *Sunday,* 24, at Wootton. Days never to be forgot!

Monday, July 25. I heard at Oxford that Charles Graves had been carried away by his friends, as stark mad.

Thursday, July 28. I spied Robinson and Bateley in the Long-walk, and crossed over to speak with them. They fell upon me unawares, desiring me to take some of the Cowley saints to Georgia; charged the Methodists with in trusion, schism, and bringing neglect upon the ministry. We differed *toto coelo.* I left them with, Remember, you will be of my mind when you come to die.

Friday, July 29. We set out for London, with Mr. Morgan and Mr. Kinchin; and on

Saturday, July 30, finished our travels at College Street, where I had the satisfaction of finding my old hearty friend, Benjamin Ingham.

Monday, August 1. I read Mr. Oglethorpe my brother's letter to the Trustees, charging Horton with raising a scandalous report about me. He would not advise one way or the other: which I interpreted as a dissuasive, and therefore took no farther notice of the matter.

Wednesday, August 17. After spending some time at Hatfield, I set out with my brother Lambert for London. At Epping he went back, full of good resolutions.

Thursday, August 18. Hearing that Mrs. Delamotte was now in town, I went to see her. We fell into discourse upon resignation; and she seemed resolved to acquiesce in the will of God, detaining her Isaac from her.

Sunday, August 21. I took horse again for Hatfield; read prayers, and preached at Wormley; called on Dr. Nichols, and rode on. My brother I left on the 24th, in excellent temper. I called and dined at Dr. Newton's.

Thursday, August 25. After giving the sacrament to a sick woman, I breakfasted with Mr. Chadwick. We had some close talk about the new birth, with which he was greatly moved. I took the opportunity of recommending regular retirement, and religious acquaintance. I preached at Ludgate, dined with

Mrs. Musgrave, and called in the afternoon at Mrs. Delamotte's. The Cambridge youth was there; but we had no very useful conversation.

Friday, August 26. I waited upon His Majesty at Hampton Court, with the Oxford Address, by the advice of Mr. Potter. The Archbishop told me he was glad to see me there. We kissed their Majesties hands, and were invited to dinner. I left that, and the company, and hasted back to town. The next day we waited upon His Royal Highness, and dined all together at St. James's.

Wednesday, August 31. I talked at large upon my state with Mr. Law, at Putney. The sum of his advice was, Renounce yourself; and be not impatient.

Friday, September 9. I consulted Mr. Law a second time, and asked him several questions: 'With what comment shall I read the Scriptures?' 'None.' 'What do you think of one who dies unrenewed, while endeavouring after it?' 'It concerns neither you to ask, nor me to answer.' 'Shall I write once more to such a person?' 'No.' 'But I am persuaded it will do him good.' 'Sir, I have told you my opinion.' 'Shall I write to you?' 'Nothing I can either speak or write will do you any good.'

Saturday, September 10. Calling at Mr. Delamotte's, I found Miss Hetty there, and gave her her brother's letter. We soon fell into talk about the new birth. She lamented her not being acquainted with me sooner; and that she could not be in the country now I was going thither. I walked back to Charles Rivington's, and fetched her Mr. Law; and then took coach for Eltham and Blendon. My friend Benjamin had been there before me, and met with such a reception as encouraged me to follow. He had preached to them with power; and still more powerfully by his life and conversation. The eldest sister, and Cambridge scholar, were struck to the heart. The first evening passed in discourse of my name sake in America.

Sunday, September 11. I preached the one thing needful: had some serious talk with Miss Betsy, and read to Mrs. Delamotte part of my Journal, relating to their intended visitant, Appee.

Monday, September 12. I returned to town, and spent an hour with Hetty, in discoursing on the inward change, and reading Law. She received all his sayings with the utmost readiness.

Tuesday, September 13. I went again to my simple Hetty, to learn some of her humility. Her convictions were much deepened by my reading the *Life of God in the Soul of Man*. I took my leave, and set out for Oxford, by way of Windsor, and Mr. Thorold's.

Thursday, September 15 I rose (at Sarney's) with earnest desires of resigning myself up entirely to God. I had the satisfaction of seeing an excellent letter from young Graves in the country.

Friday, September 16. I walked over with Mr. Gambold to Stanton Harcourt. After much talk of their states, we agreed that I should not speak at all to my sister on religion, but fully to his.

Calling accidentally in the evening at my sister Kezia's room, she fell upon my neck, and in a flood of tears begged me to pray for her. Seeing her so softened, I did not know but this might be her time, and sat down. She anticipated me, by saying she had felt here what she never felt before, and believed now there was such a thing as the new creature. She was full of earnest wishes for divine love; owned there was a depth in religion she had never fathomed; that she was not, but longed to be, converted; would give up all to obtain the love of God; renewed her request with great vehemence that I would pray for her; often repeating, 'I am weak, I am exceeding weak.' I prayed over her, and blessed God from my heart; then used Pascal's prayer for conversion, with which she was much affected, and begged me to write it out for her. After supper (at which I could not eat for joy), I read Mr. Law's account of Redemption. She was greatly moved, full of tears and sighs, and eagerness for more. Poor Mrs. Gambold was quite unaffected, her time being not yet come.

Saturday, September 17. I prayed with Kez., still in the same temper; convinced all her misery had proceeded from her not loving God.

This morning Mr. Wells, of Jesus College, came in. I took occasion to mention Mr. Law on the Redemption; read part of it, and rejoiced in his so cordially joining us.

Sunday, September 18. I preached at the Castle, and gave the sacrament to threescore communicants. In the afternoon at Stanton Harcourt. I was continually called upon by Kez., to pray with her. We supped at Mr. Bonnel's.

Wednesday, September 21. I rejoiced to hear at Oxford that Graves was returned from his friends unshaken. At night he came in (to Sarney's), fell upon my neck, and burst into tears. It is hard to say whether his friends' hatred, or his love, of me exceeds.

Thursday, September 22. I breakfasted with Mr. Rock at Nuneham; and dined at Maple Durham with Mr. Burton. Next morning I got to Mr. Thorold's, at Windsor; and in two hours to London. But my hard riding had nearly occasioned my being apprehended for an highwayman.

Saturday, September 24. At twelve I set out for Blendon. Passing Mr. Delamotte's, I was minded to call, though they were all out of town. Contrary to my expectation, I found Hetty left behind. We passed two hours in conference and prayer. Two hours afterwards I was with her again, and read Scougal on 'Few saved.' She was quite melted down, and, after a prayer for love, said, 'God knows my heart: I do desire nothing but Him.'

Sunday, September 25. I met her at the sacrament in Crooked Lane, and endeavoured to prepare her for persecution, which all must suffer who will live godly in Christ Jesus.

Tuesday, September 27. I rode to Windsor; and next day to Maple Durham by noon. An hour after I took horse, and quickly lost myself in a wood: but by breaking fences, and leaping ditches, got at last to Dorchester. I lost myself again between that and Nuneham; but soon recovered it, and by night came to honest Mr. Sarney's.

Thursday, September 29. I found Graves and Kezzy still pressing forward. In the afternoon I met Mr. Wells alone, and had some close talk with him upon the new birth, self-renunciation, &c. He confessed reputation was his idol; rejected his own righteousness, convinced, but fearful, longing to break loose. I went with him to the chapel; and afterwards resumed the subject. He seemed on the brink of the new birth.

Saturday, October 1. I prayed by Mr. Carter, who lay a-dying: and by Mrs. Sarney, in the same condition.

Sunday, October 2. I carried Graves to Stanton Harcourt, where I gave the sacrament, and then preached at Southleigh. In the evening we returned to Oxford.

Monday, October 3. At six I took horse for Barkswell. A little on this side Banbury my horse threw me, with great violence, over his head, and tumbled after, but not upon me. I rose first, unhurt, except that I sprained my leg. With much wandering through excessive bad roads, by night I got to Mr. Boyse's, quite exhausted.

Tuesday, October 4. I waked much refreshed. The family showed me all possible civility, especially dear Susan, for whose sake I had come.

Wednesday, October 5. We parted as friends should part. I returned, before night, to Oxford.

Friday, October 7. I received a letter from James Hutton, summoning me on board in fourteen days.

Saturday, October 8. I endeavoured to fix Kinchin, Sarney, Washington, and Hutchins in meeting as my brother, &c., used formerly. I rode to Spilsbury, to see my old friend Horn, and returned by night to read Nicodemus at Queen's.

Sunday, October 9. I gave the sacrament, and preached at Southleigh. In the evening at dear Charles's; still growing in humility and love.

Monday, October 10. Being determined not to leave England till I had come to a full explanation with Dicky Graves, this morning I went to his rooms, talked the whole matter over, and were both entirely satisfied. Then I spoke of my making his brother Charles mad; hoped he him self would be one of those whose life fools count madness; explained the nature of true religion; 'no other than what you once laboured after, till the gentleman swallowed up the Christian.' He was greatly moved; complained he could not pray. I appealed to him whether he had not formerly felt more solid pleasure in religion than in all the caresses of the world. He confessed it, and resolved to return. I earnestly recommended Law, and daily retirement, as my last legacy. 'My heart's desire to God for you is, that you may be saved. In a little time, all I can do will be to pray for you: and I hope you will now pray for me, as for a friend, not an enemy.' He answered, 'That I shall do heartily. I am satisfied you are my sincere friend.' We then kissed, and parted till that day.

Tuesday, October 11. I set out for London. In a mile's riding my horse fell lame. I sung the 91st Psalm, and put myself under the divine protection. I had scarce ended, and turned the hut, on Shotover Hill, when a man came up to me, and demanded my money, showing, but not presenting, a pistol. I gave him my purse. He asked how much there was. 'About thirty shillings.' 'Have you no more?' 'I will see;' put my hand in my pocket, and gave him some halfpence. He repeated the question, 'Have you no more?' I had thirty pounds in a private pocket; bade him search himself; which he did not choose. He ordered me to dismount, which I did; but begged hard for my horse again, promising not to pursue him. He took my word, and restored him. I rode gently on, praising God. My bags, and watch, and gold, the robber was *forced* to leave me. By the evening I reached Westminster.

Friday, October 14. I was informed at the office that I was to go in three weeks with the Lieutenant-Colonel by way of Gibraltar.

Sunday, October 16. I rode to Blendon, and read S.S. to the two sisters, and prayed with them for conversion. I was employed again in like manner, after the opposers were gone to bed.

Tuesday, October 18. Jacky Delamotte and I took horse. Mine fell into a hole; but I kept my seat. His followed, and flung him over his head. Neither was hurt.

Friday, October 28. I found Miss Betty at Fresh Wharf, and spent an hour or two with her and Jacky. Next morning I was with her alone, and spoke largely of the danger of lukewarmness, and resting in negative goodness. I never saw her so moved before.

Sunday, October 30. I waked them at five, and attended them to Forster Lane, where we heard Mr. Whitefield, and communicated together. I preached at St. Helen's the one thing needful. In the afternoon I carried her and her brother to Mr. Chadwick's (my usual lodgings), and thence to Ironmonger's Lane. After preaching the same sermon here, we drank tea at Mr. Chadwick's, and then took coach for College Street. They were much delighted with the singing there, and edified, I hope, by George Whitefield's example. It was near eleven before I left them at their own house.

Wednesday, November 2. I was at the office, and returned the Trustees thanks for the 50 they had lately ordered me, as a missionary. I dined with them; and they desired me to draw up a scheme for an Orphan-house. The evening I passed at Fresh Wharf: good old Mr. Delamotte was there, and pleased me much by his seeming so heartily to relish our reading Bishop Hall.

Friday, November 4. I heard an excellent sermon at St. Antholin's, on holiness, or likeness to God; and passed the evening with B. Delamotte; who then told me the reason why I was not sent for to Blendon was Mrs. Delamotte's fear of my making Hetty run mad: and when I gave them notice of my coming, she sent her up to town, that I might not see her; which Providence made the means of my having so many hours with her alone.

Saturday, November 5. I met and turned back with Betty, to hear Mr. Whitefield preach, not with the persuasive words of man's wisdom, but with the demonstration of the Spirit and with power. The churches will not contain the multitudes that throng to hear him.

Monday, November 7. I read over *Pietas Hallensis;* and desired our Orphan-house might be begun in the power of faith.

Thursday, November 10. In obedience to a summons from Miss Betsy this morning, I took coach for Greenwich, and walked the rest of the way to Blendon. We had some animating discourse before Mrs. Delamotte came in. Then we fell into talk of the new birth, which she did not at all relish; but continued still cold, averse, and prejudiced against the truth.

Sunday, November 13. I preached at Bexley, on the love of God. Mrs. Delamotte thanked me for my sermon with tears; owned she had loved Charles too well; and was quite altered in her behaviour towards me. We had farther conversation on the love of God. Mr. Delamotte confessed there could be no happiness in anything else.

Monday, November 14. Little Molly burst into tears upon my telling her God loved her. The whole family now appear not far from the kingdom of God.

Sunday, November 20. At St. Helen's I preached the circumcision of heart. The next day my flux returned.

Tuesday, November 22. Mr. Oglethorpe advised me to go to Tiverton. I went to take my leave of our friends at Blendon. Mrs. Delamotte was quite open, and not afraid that her son should be called a Methodist.

Friday, November 25. At Mrs. Hutton's this evening, my brothers Lambert and Wright visited me. The latter has corrupted the former, after all the pains I have taken with him, and brought him back to drinking. I was full, yet could not speak; prayed for meekness, and then set before him the things he had done, in the devil's name, toward re-converting a soul to him. He left us abruptly. I encouraged poor J. Lambert to turn again unto God.

Monday, November 28. I took coach for Tiverton. The next day I called on my mother in Salisbury. She vehemently protested against our returning to Georgia.

Wednesday, November 30. I had much serious conversation with a gentlewoman in the coach concerning the new birth. I read part of Mr. Law. She was deeply struck, melted, conquered.

Thursday, December 1. We lodged at Dorchester, when my distemper fully returned.

Friday, December 2. I met horses at Honiton, and by four came to Tiverton; where I found my brother much better.

Sunday, December 4. I was much melted at the sacrament. In the evening I reproved my sister (which I am often forced to do) for evil-speaking.

Thursday, December 22. Quite wearied out by her incessant slanders, to-day I had a downright quarrel with her about it. My brother on these occasions is either silent or on my side.

Tuesday, December 27. I was not sorry to set out for London. I rode as far as Taunton.

Wednesday, December 28. In the coach I employed myself mostly in reading Cyrus's *Travels,* and Leslie's *Short Method with the Deists.*

Thursday, December 29. We narrowly escaped overturning, through the loss of a wheel. I supped in Salisbury, at my brother Hall's.

Saturday, December 31. I set out at two in the morning, and with the night came to James Hutton's.

[1] Dr. Stephen Hales, one of the Trustees for the colony of Georgia, was born September 7, 1677, and was educated at Cambridge. The University of Oxford conferred upon him the degree of D.D. He held the living of Portlock, in Somersetshire, and that of Farringdon, in Hampshire, with the perpetual curacy of Teddington, near Twickenham, in Middlesex, where he resided, and was visited by persons of rank and science, who sought his society; among whom was Frederick Prince of Wales, to whose widow, the Princess Dowager, Dr. Hales was made Clerk of the Closet. He died at Teddington, January 4, 1761, where he was buried. A handsome monument to his memory was erected by the Princess Dowager of Wales, in Westminster Abbey, near that of Handel. His *Vegetable Staticks,* in two volumes, passed through several editions, and was translated into French, Italian, German, and Dutch. A curious and valuable extract from it will be found in Dr. Adam Clarke's Commentary on Gen. iii. 18. - T. JACKSON.

1738

Thursday, January 5. I made frequent visits this month to Blendon, and rejoiced over Mrs. Delamotte, now entirely cordial and friendly. We were joined by Mr. Piers, the minister of Bexley, who delighted in every opportunity of conversing, singing, and praying with us.

Friday, February 3. In the afternoon news was brought me at James Hutton's, that my brother was come from America. I could not believe, till at night I saw him. He comes, not driven away, but to tell the true state of the colony; which, according to his account, is truly deplorable.

Saturday, February 4. I informed Mr. Oglethorpe of his arrival. He was very inquisitive into the cause of his coming; said he ought not to have returned without the Trustees leave. At ten, before the Council, I heard the fresh pleadings for Carolina.

Monday, February 6. I waited on the good Archbishop, who received me with his usual kindness.

Wednesday, February 8. I was with the Trustees, who were surprised by my brother's account of Georgia, the fewness of the people, &c.

Friday, February 10. We dined at Mr. Vernon's, who accosted me, 'Well, sir, I hope you intend returning to Georgia.' I answered, 'That is my desire and design.' I heard more of the great discouragements the poor people labour under.

Saturday, February 11. I heard Clerk plead for Georgia, before the Council, and Mr. Oglethorpe's speech.

Thursday, February 16. Mr. Oglethorpe told me, 'Your brother must have a care. There is a very strong spirit raising against him. People say he is come over to do mischief to the colony. He will be called upon for his reasons, why he left the people.' I answered, 'Sir, he has been twice before at the Board for that purpose, but was not asked that question, and therefore had no opportunity to answer it. We will attend them again on Wednesday morning.' I waited on his Lordship of London, and informed him of my brother's return. He spoke honourably of him; expressed a great desire to see him; asked many questions about Georgia and the Trustees; forgot his usual reserve, and dismissed me very kindly.

Friday, February 17. I came in the Oxford coach to my old lodgings at Mr. Sarney's.

Saturday, February 18. I rode over to Stanton Harcourt, to see John Gambold and my sister. My brother met us. We prayed and sang together. In the evening I prayed at Mr. Sarney's, with some scholars, and a Moravian.

Sunday, February 19. I received the sacrament once more at Christ Church.

Monday, February 20. I began teaching Peter Bohler English.

Tuesday, February 21. In the afternoon I lay down, half distracted with the tooth-ache.

Wednesday, February 22. I waked much better. At five I had some close conversation with Peter Böhler, who pressed upon our scholars the necessity of combining, and instanced in many awakened, but fallen asleep again, for want of it. He talked much of the necessity of prayer and faith.

Friday, February 24. At six in the evening, an hour after I had taken my electuary, the tooth ache returned more violently than ever. I smoked tobacco; which set me a-vomiting, and took away my senses and pain together. At eleven I waked in extreme pain, which I thought would quickly separate soul and body. Soon after Peter Böhler came to my bedside. I asked him to pray for me. He seemed unwilling at first, but, beginning very faintly, he raised his voice by degrees, and prayed for my recovery with strange confidence. Then he took me by the hand, and calmly said, 'You will not die now.' I thought within myself, 'I cannot hold out in this pain till morning. If it abates before, I believe I may recover.' He asked me, 'Do you hope to be saved?' 'Yes.' 'For what reason do you hope it?' 'Because I have used my best endeavours to serve God.' He shook his head, and said no more. I thought him very uncharitable, saying in my heart, 'What, are not my endeavours a sufficient ground of hope? Would he rob me of my endeavours? I have nothing else to trust to.'

By the morning my pain was moderated. Ted Bentham, calling, then persuaded me to be blooded. I continued in great pain. In the evening he brought Dr. Manaton. On Saturday morning I was blooded again; and at night a third time.

Sunday, February 26. Mr. Wells brought my sister Kezzy. Dr. Fruin came. I dictated a letter to Dr. Cockburn, and James Hutton.

Monday, February 27. The scale seemed to turn for life. I had prayed that my pains might not outlast this day; and was answered.

Tuesday, February 28. My dear James Hutton came post from London, and brought me Dr. Cockburn's letter and directions. As soon as I was able, I sent my brother at Tiverton the following account:

"Dear Brother, I borrow another's hand, as I cannot use my own. You remember Dr. South's saying [I have been within the jaws of death, but he was not suffered to shut his mouth upon me]. I ought never to forget it. Dr. Manaton told me he expected to have found me dead at his second visit. This several remarkable accidents concurred to hinder. I had kept in a week before the pleurisy came, and taken physic twice. At midnight it seized me so violently, that I never expected to see the morning. In the preceding afternoon I had taken Dr. Cockburn's electuary, and an hour after was visited by so outrageous a tooth-ache, that it forced me to the abominable remedy of a pipe. This quickly made me discharge my astringent, and, in all probability, saved my life, binding medicines being poison in a pleuritic fever. I took my illness for the flux, and so never thought of sending for a physician. T. Bentham fetched him against my will, and was probably the instrument of saving my life a second time. Dr. Manaton called in Dr. Fruin. They bled me three times, and poured down draughts, oils, and apozems without end. For four days the balance was even. Then, as Spenser says,

> I over-wrestled my strong enemy.

Ever since I have been slowly gathering strength; and yesterday took my first journey to my sister's room, who has been with me from the beginning, and no small comfort to me.

'One consequence of my sickness you will not be sorry for, its stopping my sudden return to Georgia. For the doctor tells me to undertake a voyage now would be certain death. Some reasons for *his* not going immediately my brother will mention to you in person.

'Before I was taken ill, my brother set out for Tiverton, but came back instead of proceeding on his journey; stayed a week with me, and then went with Mr. Kinchin to Manchester.

'For some days that I continued mending, I was greatly tormented with the tooth-ache. One day I prayed that the pain might be suspended; and it was for all that day.

'I had Dr. Fruin to my sister, taken ill. We communicated almost every day.'

Tuesday, March 28. I was greatly moved in reading the *Life of Mr. Halyburton.*

Monday, April 3. By my brother's advice I resolved to give up my secretary's place; and to-day wrote my letter of resignation.

Saturday, April 8. I got abroad to the evening prayers at Christ Church; and received comfort from the lessons and anthem.

Wednesday, April 12. I received Mr. Oglethorpe's answer to my letter of resignation; wherein he offered, if I would keep my place, to get it supplied in my absence by a deputy.

Saturday, April 15. Drs. Fruin and Manaton called, and forbad my voyage. Both as physicians and friends they advised me not to go, but stay at College, since I might, as senior Master, expect offices and preferment.

Wednesday, April 19. I came up to town, to take my leave of Mr. Oglethorpe, who received me with his accustomed kindness. The next day I had the satisfaction of once more meeting that man of God, Peter Böhler.

Monday, April 24. I took a ride to Blendon. In the afternoon we made Mr. Piers a visit; and returning, found Mr. Broughton and my brother at Blendon.

Tuesday, April 25. Soon after five, as we were met in our little chapel, Mrs. Delamotte came to us. We sang, and fell into a dispute whether conversion was gradual or instantaneous. My brother was very positive for the latter, and very shocking; mentioned some late instances of gross sinners believing in a moment. I was much offended at his worse than unedifying discourse. Mrs. Delamotte left us abruptly. I stayed, and insisted a man need not know when first he had faith. His obstinacy in favouring the contrary opinion drove me at last out of the room. Mr. Broughton was only not so much scandalized as myself. After dinner he and my brother returned to town. I stayed behind, and read them the *Life of Mr. Halyburton:* one instance, but only one, of instantaneous conversion.

Wednesday, April 26. I passed the day at Mr. Piers's, in singing, and reading, and mutual encouragement. In the evening we finished Halyburton. The meltingness it occasioned in me (like those before), soon passed away as a morning cloud. Next morning I returned to London.

Friday, April 28. No sooner was I got to James Button's, having removed my things thither from his father's, than the pain in my side returned, and with that my fever. Having disappointed God in His last visitation, He has now again brought me to the bed of sickness. To wards midnight I received some relief by bleeding. In the morning Dr. Cockburn came to see me; and a better physician, Peter Bohler, whom God had detained in England for my good. He stood by my bedside, and prayed over me, that now at least I might see the divine intention in this and my late illness. I immediately thought it might be that I should again consider Bohler's doctrine of faith; examine myself whether I was in the faith; and if I was not, never cease seeking and longing after it till I attained it.

Monday, May 1. Mr. Piers called to see me. I exhorted him to labour after that faith which he thinks I have, and I know I have not. After receiving the sacrament, I felt a small anticipation of peace, and said, Now I have demonstration against the Moravian doctrine that a man cannot have peace without assurance of his pardon. I now have peace, yet cannot say of a surety that my sins are forgiven. The next and several times after that I received the sacrament, I had not so much as bare attention, God no longer trusting me with comfort, which I should immediately turn against Himself.

For some days following I felt a faint longing for faith; and could pray for nothing else. My desires were quickened by a letter of Mr. Edmunds, seeking

Christ as in an agony.

Saturday, May 6. God still kept up the little spark of desire, which He Himself had enkindled in me; and I seemed determined to speak of, and wish for, nothing but faith in Christ. Yet could not this preserve me from sin; which I this day ran into with my eyes open; so that after ten years vain struggling, I own and feel it absolutely unconquerable. By bearing witness to the truth before Miss Delamotte, Mr. Baldwyn, and others, I found my desires of apprehending Christ increased.

Thursday, May 11. I was just going to remove to old Mr. Button's, when God sent Mr. Bray to me, a poor ignorant mechanic, who knows nothing but Christ; yet by knowing Him, knows and discerns all things. Some time ago I had taken leave of Peter Böhler, confessed my unbelief and want of forgiveness, but declared my firm persuasion that I should receive the atonement before I died. His answer was, Be it unto thee according to thy faith.

Mr. Bray is now to supply Böhler's place. We prayed together for faith. I was quite over powered and melted into tears, and hereby induced to think it was God's will that I should go to his house, and not to Mr. Hutton's. He was of the same judgement. Accordingly I was carried thither in a chair.

His sister I found in earnest pursuit of Christ; his wife well inclined to conversion. I had not been here long, when Mr. Broughton called. I hoped to find him altered like myself; but, alas! his time is not yet come. As to Mrs. Turner, he gave her up; 'but for you, Mrs. Bray,' said he, 'I hope you are still in your senses, and not run mad after a faith which must be felt.' He went on contradicting and blaspheming. I thought it my duty to withstand him, and to confess my want of faith. 'God help you, poor man,' he replied: 'if I could think you have not faith, I am sure it would drive me to despair.' I put all my hopes of ever attaining it, or eternal salvation, upon the truth of this assertion, *'I have not now the faith of the gospel.'*

As soon as he left us, Mr. Bray read me many comfortable scriptures, which greatly strengthened my desire; so that I was persuaded I should not leave his house before I believed with my heart unto righteousness.

Friday, May 12. I waked in the same blessed temper, hungry and thirsty after God. I began Isaiah, and seemed to see that to me were the promises made, and would be fulfilled, for that Christ loved me. I found myself more desirous, more assured I should believe. This day (and indeed my whole time) I spent in discoursing on faith, either with those that had it, or those that sought it; in reading the Scripture, and in prayer.

I was much moved at the sight of Mr. Ainsworth, a man of great learning, above seventy, who, like old Simeon, was waiting to see the Lord's salvation, that he might depart in peace. His tears, and vehemence, and childlike simplicity, showed him upon the entrance of the kingdom of heaven. In the afternoon I read Isaiah with Air. Edmunds: saw him full of promises, and that they belonged to me. In the midst of our reading, Miss Claggetts came, and asked that they might hear us. We were all much encouraged to pursue the glorious prize held out to us by the evangelical prophet.

When the company was gone, I joined with Mr. Bray in prayer and the Scripture, and was so greatly affected, that I almost thought Christ was coming that moment. I concluded the night with private vehement prayer.

Saturday, May 13. I waked without Christ; yet still desirous of finding Him. Soon after W. Delamotte came, and read me the 68th Psalm, strangely full of comfortable promises. Toward noon I was enabled to pray with desire and hope, and to lay claim to the promises in general. The afternoon I spent with my friends, in mutual exhortation to wait patiently for the Lord in prayer and reading. At night my brother came, exceeding heavy. I forced him (as he had often forced me) to sing an hymn to Christ, and almost thought He would come while we were singing: assured He would come quickly. At *night* I received much light and comfort from the Scriptures.

Sunday, May 14. The beginning of the day I was very heavy, weary, and unable to pray; but the desire soon returned, and I found much comfort both in prayer and in the Word, my eyes being opened more and more to discern and lay hold on the promises. I longed to find Christ, that I might show Him to all mankind; that I might praise, that I might love Him.

Several persons called to-day, and were convinced of unbelief. Some of them afterwards went to Mr. Broughton, and were soon made as easy as Satan and their own hearts could wish.

Monday, May 15. I finished Halyburton's Life with Miss Claggetts, &c. I found comfort in the 102nd Psalm.

Tuesday, May 16. I waked weary, faint, and heartless. My brother Hall coming to see me, I urged him to examine himself, whether he was in the faith. Two questions decided the matter: Are you sure that is light? Yes. Are you as sure of the things unseen; of Christ being in you of a truth? Yes; infinitely surer. In the afternoon I seemed deeply sensible of my misery, in being without Christ.

Wednesday, May 17. I experienced the power of Christ rescuing me in temptation. To-day I first saw Luther on the Galatians, which Mr. Holland had accidentally lit upon. We began, and found him nobly full of faith. My friend, in hearing him, was so affected as to breathe out sighs and groans unutterable. I marvelled that we were so soon and so entirely removed from Him that called us into the grace of Christ, unto another gospel. Who would believe our Church had been founded on this important article of justification by faith alone? I am astonished I should ever think this a new doctrine; especially while our Articles and Homilies stand unrepealed, and the key of knowledge is not yet taken away.

From this time I endeavoured to ground as many of our friends as came in this fundamental truth, salvation by faith alone, not an idle, dead faith, but a faith which works by love, and is necessarily productive of all good works and all holiness.

I spent some hours this evening in private with Martin Luther, who was greatly blessed to me, especially his conclusion of the 2nd chapter. I laboured, waited, and prayed to feel 'who loved *me*, and gave Himself for *me*.' When nature, near exhausted, forced me to bed, I opened the book upon 'For He will finish the work, and cut it short in righteousness, because a short work will the Lord make upon earth.' After this comfortable assurance that He would come, and would not tarry, I slept in peace.

Thursday, May 18. In the approach of a temptation, I looked up to Christ, and confessed my helplessness. The temptation was immediately beat down, and continually kept off by a power not my own. About midnight I was waked by the return of my pleurisy. I felt great pain and straitness at my heart; but found immediate relief by bleeding. I had some discourse with Mr. Bray; thought myself willing to die the next moment, if I might but believe this; but was sure I could not die till I did believe. I earnestly desired it.

Friday, May 19. At five this morning the pain and difficulty in breathing returned. The surgeon was sent for; but I fell asleep before he could bleed me a second time. I was easier all day, after taking Dr. Cockburn's medicines. I had not much desire. I received the sacrament; but not Christ. At seven Mrs. Turner came, and told me I should not rise from that bed till I believed. I believed her saying, and asked, 'Has God then bestowed faith upon you?' 'Yes, He has.' 'Why, have you peace with God?' 'Yes, perfect peace.' 'And do you love Christ above all things?' 'I do, above all things incomparably.' 'Then you are willing to die?' 'I am; and would be glad to die this moment; for I know all my sins are blotted out; the handwriting that was against me is taken out of the way, and nailed to His cross. He has saved me by His death; He has washed me with His blood; He has hid me in His wounds. I have peace in Him, and rejoice with joy unspeakable, and full of glory.'

Her answers were so full to these and the most searching questions I could ask, that I had no doubt of her having received the atonement; and -waited for it myself with a more assured hope. Feeling an anticipation of joy upon her account, and thanking Christ as I could, I looked for Him all night with prayers and sighs and unceasing desires.

Saturday, May 20. I waked much disappointed, and continued all day in great dejection, which the sacrament did not in the least abate. Nevertheless God would not suffer me to doubt the truth of His promises. Mr. Bray, too, seemed troubled at my not yet believing, and complained of his uneasiness and want of patience. But so it is with me, says he; when my faith begins to fail, God gives me some sign to support it. He then opened a Testament, and read the first words that presented, Matt. ix. 1: 'And He entered into a ship, and passed over, and came into His own city. And, behold, they brought to Him a man sick of the palsy, lying on a bed: and Jesus, seeing their faith, said unto the sick of the palsy, Son, be of good cheer; thy sins be forgiven thee. And, behold, certain of the scribes and Pharisees said within themselves, This man blasphemeth. And Jesus, knowing their thoughts, said, Wherefore think ye evil in your hearts? For whether is easier, to say, Thy sins be forgiven thee, or to say, Arise and walk? But that ye may know that the Son of Man hath power on earth to forgive sins, (then saith He to the sick of the palsy,) Arise, take up thy bed, and go unto thine own house. And he arose, and departed to his house. And when the multitude saw it, they marvelled, and glorified God, which had given such power unto man.'

It was a long while before he could read this through, for tears of joy: and I saw herein, and firmly believed, that his faith would be available for the healing of me.

The Day of Pentecost

Sunday, May 21, 1738. I waked in hope and expectation of His coming. At nine my brother and some friends came, and sang an hymn to the Holy Ghost. My comfort and hope were hereby increased. In about half an hour they went: I betook myself to prayer; the substance as follows: 'O Jesus, Thou hast said, "I will come unto you"; Thou hast said, "I will send the Comforter unto you"; Thou hast said, "My Father and I will come unto you, and make our abode with you." Thou art God who canst not lie; I wholly rely upon Thy most true promise: accomplish it in Thy time and manner.' Having said this, I was composing myself to sleep, in quietness and peace, when I heard one come in (Mrs. Musgrave, I thought, by the voice) and say, 'In the name of Jesus of Nazareth, arise, and I believe, and thou shalt be healed of all thy infirmities.' I wondered how it should enter into her head to speak in that manner. The words struck me to the heart. I sighed, and said within myself, 'Oh that Christ would but speak thus to me!' I lay musing and trembling: then thought, But what if it should be Him? I will send at least to see. I rang, and, Mrs. Turner coming, I desired her to send up Mrs. Musgrave. She went down, and, returning, said, Mrs. Musgrave has not been here. My heart sunk within me at the word, and I hoped it might be Christ indeed. However, I sent her down again to inquire, and felt in the meantime a strange palpitation of heart. I said, yet feared to say, 'I believe, I believe!' She came up again and said, 'It was I, a weak, sinful creature, spoke; but the words were Christ's: He commanded me to say them, and so constrained me that I could not forbear.'

I sent for Mr. Bray, and asked him whether I believed. He answered, I ought not to doubt of it: it was Christ spoke to me. He knew it; and willed us to pray together: 'but first,' said he, 'I will read what I have casually opened upon: "Blessed is the man whose unrighteousness is forgiven, and whose sin is covered: blessed is the man to whom the Lord imputeth no sin, and in whose spirit is no guile."' Still I felt a violent opposition and reluctance to believe; yet still the Spirit of God strove with my own and the evil spirit, till by degrees He chased away the darkness of my unbelief. I found myself convinced, I knew not how nor when; and immediately fell to intercession.

Mr. Bray then told me, his sister had been ordered by Christ to come and say those words to me. This she afterwards confirmed, and related to me more at large the manner of her believing. At night, and nearly the moment I was taken ill, she dreamt she heard one knock at the door: she went down, and opened it; saw a person in white; caught hold of and asked him who he was; was answered, 'I am Jesus Christ,' and cried out, with great vehemence, 'Come in, come in!'

She waked in a fright. It was immediately suggested to her, 'You must not mind this: it is all a dream, an illusion.' She continued wavering and uneasy all Friday till evening prayers. No sooner were they begun than she found herself full of the power of faith, so that she could scarce contain herself, and almost doubted whether she was sober. At the same time she was enlarged in love and prayer for all mankind, and commanded to go and assure me from Christ of my recovery, soul and body. She returned home repeating with all joy and triumph, 'I believe, I believe': yet her heart failed her, and she durst not say the words to me that night.

On Sunday morning she took Mr. Bray aside, burst into tears, and informed him of the matter; objecting she was a poor weak sinful creature, and should she go to a minister? She could not do it; nor rest till she did. He asked whether she had ever found herself so before. 'No, never.' 'Why, then,' said he, 'go. Remember Jonah. You declare promises, not threatenings. Go in the name of the Lord. Fear not your own weakness. Speak you the words: Christ will do the work. Out of the mouth of babes and sucklings hath He ordained strength.'

They prayed together, and she then went up, but durst not come in till she had prayed again by herself. About six minutes after she had left him, he found and felt, while she was speaking the words, that Christ was with us. I never heard words uttered with like solemnity. The sound of her voice was entirely changed into that of Mrs. Musgrave. (If I can be sure of anything sensible.) I rose and looked into the Scripture. The words that first presented were, 'And now, Lord, what is my hope? truly my hope is even in Thee.' I then cast down my eye, and met, 'He hath put a new song in my mouth, even a thanksgiving unto our God. Many shall see it, and fear, and shall put their trust in the Lord.' Afterwards I opened upon Isa. xl. 1: 'Comfort ye, comfort ye My people, saith your God: speak ye comfortably to Jerusalem, and cry unto her, that her warfare is accomplished, that her iniquity is pardoned; for she hath received of the Lord's hand double for all her sin.'

I now found myself at peace with God, and rejoiced in hope of loving Christ. My temper for the rest of the day was, mistrust of my own great, but before unknown, weakness. I saw that by faith I stood; by the continual support of faith, which kept me from falling, though of myself I am ever sinking into sin. I went to bed still sensible of my own weakness (I humbly hope to be more and more so), yet confident of Christ's protection.

Monday, May 22. Under His protection I waked next morning, and rejoiced in reading the 107th Psalm, so nobly describing what God had done for my soul. I fell asleep again, and waked out of a dream that I was fighting with two devils; had one under my feet; the other faced me some time, but faded, and sunk, and vanished away, upon my telling him I belonged to Christ.

To-day I saw Him chiefly as my King, and found Him in His power: but saw little of the love of Christ crucified, or of my sins past; though more, I humbly hope, of my own weakness and His strength. I had many evil thoughts darted into my mind, but I rejected them immediately (yet not I). At noon I rose, continually fainting, nevertheless upheld. I was greatly strengthened by Isa. xliii., which God directed me to: 'But now thus saith the Lord that created thee, O Jacob, and He that formed thee, O Israel, Fear not: for I have redeemed thee, I have called thee by thy name; thou art Mine. When thou passest through the waters, I will be with thee; and through the rivers, they shall not overflow thee: when thou walkest through the fire, thou shalt not be burned; neither shall the flame kindle upon thee. For I am the Lord thy God, the Holy One of Israel, thy Saviour.'

My brother coming, we joined in intercession for him. In the midst of prayer, I almost believed the Holy Ghost was coming upon him. In the evening we sang and prayed again. I found myself very weak in body, but thought I ought to pray for my friends, being the only priest among them. I kneeled down, and was immediately strengthened, both mind and body. The enemy did not lose such an opportunity of tempting me to pride: but, God be praised, my strength did I ascribe unto Him. I was often since assisted to pray readily and earnestly, without a form. Not unto me, Lord, not unto me, but to Thy Name be the glory!

An old friend called to see me, under great apprehensions that I was running mad. His fears were not a little increased by my telling him the prayer of faith had healed me when sick at Oxford. 'He looked to see the rays of light about my head,' he said, and more to that purpose. I begged him, for his own sake, not to pass sentence till he had his full evidence concerning me. This he could not promise, but faintly prayed me to flee from London, and, in despair of me, took his leave.

It was morning before I could get to sleep. Many motions of pride arose, and were continually beaten down by Christ my King. The devil also tempted me to impatience through pain; but God turned it into an occasion of resignation.

Tuesday, May 23. I waked under the protection of Christ, and gave myself up, soul and body, to Him. At nine I began an hymn upon my conversion, but was persuaded to break off, for fear of pride. Mr. Bray coming, encouraged me to proceed in spite of Satan. I prayed Christ to stand by me, and finished the hymn. Upon my afterwards showing it to Mr. Bray, the devil threw in a fiery dart, suggesting that it was wrong, and I had displeased God. My heart sunk within me; when, casting my eye upon a Prayer-book, I met with an answer for him. 'Why boastest thou thyself, thou tyrant, that thou canst do mischief?' Upon this, I clearly discerned it was a device of the enemy to keep back glory from God. And it is most usual with him to preach humility when speaking will endanger his kingdom, or do honour to Christ. Least of all would he have us tell what things God has done for our souls, so tenderly does he guard us from pride. But God has showed me He can defend me from it while speaking for Him. In His name therefore,, and through His strength, I will perform my vows unto the Lord, of not hiding His righteousness within my heart, if it should ever please Him to plant it there.

Throughout this day He has kept up in me a constant sense of my own weakness. At night I was tempted to think the reason of my believing before others was my sincerity. I rejected the thought with horror, and remained more than conqueror, through Him that loved me.

Wednesday, May 24. Being to receive the sacrament to-day, I was assaulted by the fear of my old accustomed deadness; but soon recovered my confidence in Christ, that He would give me so much sense of His love now as He saw good for me. I received without any sensible devotion, much as I used to be, only that I was afterwards perfectly calm and satisfied, without doubt, fear, or scruple. Among our communicants was Mrs. Pratt, who had been with me the night before, and related her receiving Christ in a dream, when under great trouble. His words to her were, 'Be of good cheer, thy prayer is heard.' From that time to this, being six years, she has enjoyed perfect peace. Most of Saturday night she had spent in intercession for me; as on Sunday morning I experienced.

I was much pleased to-day at the sight of Mr. Ainsworth, a little child, full of grief, and fears, and love. At our repeating the line of the hymn, 'Now descend, and shake the earth,' he fell down as in an agony. I found a general delight in their singing, but little attention: yet was not disquieted.

We passed the afternoon in prayer, singing, and conference. For one half - hour I was with Miss Delamotte; now unconvinced, and full of dispute. I bore my testimony with plainness and confidence, declaring what God had done for my soul. Not hurt, but strengthened hereby.

From her I went to Miss Claggetts; young women of a better and more childlike spirit, who calmly and confidently looked for the promises. I was farther comforted by an excellent letter from my namesake in Georgia, persecuted for Christ's sake; on the highest step, I trust, of the legal state.

At eight I prayed by myself for love; with some feeling, and assurance of feeling more. Towards ten, my brother was brought in triumph by a troop of our friends, and declared, I believe. We sang the hymn with great joy, and parted with prayer. At midnight I gave myself up to Christ; assured I was safe, sleeping or waking. Had continual experience of His power to over rule all temptation; and confessed, with joy and surprise, that He was able to do exceeding abundantly for me, above what I can ask or think.

Thursday, May 25. I commended myself to Christ, my Prophet, Priest, and King. Miss D. came in a better mind. Before communicating, I left it to Christ, whether, or in what measure, He would please to manifest Himself to me, in this breaking of bread. I had no particular attention to the prayers; but in the prayer of consecration I saw, by the eye of faith, or rather, had a glimpse of, Christ's broken, mangled body as taking down from the cross. Still I could not observe the prayer, but only repeat with tears, 'O love, love!' At the same time, I felt great peace and joy; and assurance of feeling more, when it is best.

Soon after I was a little cast down, by feeling some temptation, and fore-seeing more; but God lifted me up by His word: "Fear not: for I have re-deemed thee, I have called thee by thy name; thou art Mine. When thou pass-est through the waters, I will be with thee; and through the rivers, they shall not overflow thee: when thou walkest through the fire, thou shalt not be burned; neither shall the flame kindle upon thee." (Isa. xliii.) This promise was fulfilled in me when under frequent motions of sin: I looked up to Christ, and found them beaten down continually.

Friday, May 26. We joined this morning in supplication for the poor male-factors, while passing to execution; and in the sacrament commended their souls to Christ. The great comfort we found therein made us confidently hope some of them were received as the penitent thief at the last hour. I was much refreshed soon after by Miss Delamotte, who, by the mercy of Christ, is brought back again, and more athirst after Him than ever. I dined with great liberty of spirit, being amazed to find my old enemy, intemperance, so sud-denly subdued, that I have almost forgot I was ever in bondage to him. In the evening I broke through my own great unwillingness, and at last preached faith in Christ to an accidental visitant.

Saturday, May 27. I felt a motion of anger, from a trifling disappointment; but it was no sooner felt than conquered. I received the sacrament: still no sensible love; but comfort. A gentlewoman, who has long been under the law, calling to see me, I thought, as she lived in the midst of opposers, no good could be done by speaking. Yet was I overruled to preach the Gospel. She seemed convinced and comforted. After she was gone, I was much assisted to intercede for her, and for poor Mr. Broughton, who continues the very life of all those that oppose the faith. Two or three others calling were reproved of sin by the holy Spirit of God. Miss Claggetts seemed on the very border of Canaan; being fully convinced of righteousness also, of Christ's imputed righteousness; and looking to receive it every moment as by promise theirs.

Trinity Sunday, May 28. I rose in great heaviness, which neither private nor joint prayer could remove. At last I betook myself to intercession for my rela-tions, and was greatly helped and enlarged herein; particularly in prayer for a most profligate sinner. I spent the morning with James Hutton, in prayer, and singing, and rejoicing. In the afternoon my brother came, and, after a short prayer for success upon our ministry, set out for Tiverton. I then began writing my first sermon in the name of Christ my Prophet.

To-day Mrs. Bray related to me the manner of her receiving faith in public prayers, and the great conflicts she has since had with the enemy. For some days he so darkened the work of God, that though her eye of faith had been opened to see herself encompassed with the blood of Christ, yet still he suggested to her that she did not believe, because she had not the joy which others had. She was just overpowered by his devices, when in great heaviness she opened upon, 'Lord, I believe, help Thou my unbelief.' This stayed her for a time; but the tempter still pursued, and in the very words he had used to shake my brother's faith. She went to public prayers, and was fervent throughout the whole. Toward the conclusion she saw as it were Satan under her feet; and came home in all the triumph of faith.

After dinner Miss Claggett and other friends came. I thought some would be now gathered into the fold, and was much assisted to pray. I rose, and saw the younger Miss Claggett under the work of God. I asked, urged, believed that she believed. She thought so too, but was afraid to confess it. While she stood trembling and in tears, I consulted the oracle for her, and met with Isa. xxx. 18: 'And therefore will the Lord wait, that He may be gracious unto you; and there fore will He be exalted, that He may have mercy upon you: for the Lord is a God of judgement; blessed are all they that wait for Him. For the people shall dwell in Sion at Jerusalem; thou shalt weep no more: He will be very gracious to thee, at the voice of thy cry; when He shall hear it, He will answer thee.' She then opened the Book on 2 Cor. v. 17: 'Old things are passed away; behold, all things are become new. She read so far, and gave me the book to read on: And all things are of God, who hath reconciled us to Himself by Jesus Christ, and hath given to us the ministry of reconciliation; to wit, that God was in Christ, reconciling the world unto Himself, not imputing their trespasses unto them; and hath committed to us the word of reconciliation. Now then we are ambassadors for Christ, as though God did beseech you by us: we pray you in Christ's stead, be ye reconciled to God. For He hath made Him to be sin for us, who knew no sin; that we might be made the righteousness of God in Him.'

Mr. Holland then read, 'Stand fast in the liberty wherewith Christ hath made us free, and be not entangled again with the yoke of bondage.' She now openly professed her faith, and increased in confidence every moment. We joined in hearty thanks to God for His unspeakable gift. Just before parting, she opened the book upon Luke viii. 39: 'Return to thine own house, and show how great things God hath done unto thee.' This success was followed with inward trials; but at the same time I experienced the superior power of Christ.

Wednesday, May 31. To-day God enabled me, in spite of the devil and my own heart, to send Mr. Wells a plain simple account of what God hath done for my soul.

Thursday, June 1. I was troubled to-day that I could not pray, being utterly dead at the sacrament.

Friday, June 2. I was still unable to pray; still dead in communicating; full of a cowardly desire of death.

Saturday, June 3. My deadness continued, and the next day increased. I rose exceeding heavy and averse to prayer; so that I almost resolved not to go to church, which I had not been able to do till within these two or three days past. When I did go, the prayers and sacrament were exceeding grievous to me; and I could not help asking myself, 'Where is the difference between what I am now and what I was before believing?' I immediately answered, 'That the darkness was not like the former darkness, because I was satisfied there was no guilt in it; because I was assured it would be dispersed; and because, though I could not find I loved God, or feel that He loved me, yet I did and would believe He loved me notwithstanding.'

I returned home, and lay down with the same load upon me. This Mr. Ingham's coming could not alleviate. They sung, but I had no heart to join; much less in public prayers. In the evening. Mr. Brown, Holland, and others called. I was very averse to coming among them, but forced myself to it, and spent two or three hours in singing, reading, and prayer. This exercise a little revived me; and I found myself much assisted to pray.

We asked particularly that, if it was the will of God, some one might now receive the atonement. While I was yet speaking the words, Mr. Brown found power to believe. He rose and told me my prayer was heard, and answered in him. At the same time Mr. Burton opened the Bible upon Col. i. 26: 'Even the mystery which has been hid from ages and from generations, but now is made manifest to His saints; to whom God would make known what is the riches of the glory of this mystery among the Gentiles; which is Christ in you, the hope of glory.'

We were all full of joy and thanksgiving. Before we parted, I prayed with Mr. Brown, and praised God, to the great confirmation of my faith. The weight was quite taken off. I found power to pray with great earnestness, and rejoiced in my trials having continued so long, to show me that it is then the best time to labour for our neighbour, when we are most cast down, and most unable to help ourselves.

Monday, June 5. I waked thankful, with power to pray and praise. I had peace at the sacrament, and some attention in public prayer. In the afternoon I met Mrs. Sims, with Mr. and Mrs. Burton, at Islington. He told me God had given him faith, while I was praying last night; but he thought it would do hurt to declare it then. Upon finding his heart burn within him, he desired God would show him some token of his faith, and immediately opened on 'Let there be light, and there was light.' We rejoiced together in prayer and singing; and left the rest of the company much stirred up to wait for the same unspeakable gift.

Tuesday, June 6. In the evening I read Luther, as usual, to a large company of our friends. Mr. Burton was greatly affected. My inward temptations are, in a manner, uninterrupted. I never knew the energy of sin till now that I experience the superior strength of Christ.

Wednesday, June 7. I found myself this morning under my Father's protection; and reading Matt, vii., 'Ask, and ye shall receive,' I asked some sense of His love in the sacrament. It was there given me to believe assuredly that

God loved me, even when I could have no sense of it. Some imperfect perception of His love I had, and was strengthened to hope against hope, after communicating.

I went to Mrs. Sims, and passed the afternoon in singing and reading the promises. Miss Claggetts, Mr. Chapman, Verding, and others dropped in, as by accident. We all went to public prayers; whence we again returned, contrary to my intention, to Mr. Sims. We joined in pleading the promises, and asking some token for good. I rose in confidence of our prayer being heard; and at the same time Mr. Verding declared, with great simplicity and astonishment, that he had seen as it were a whole army rushing by him, and bearing the broken body of Christ. He found himself quite over powered at the sight; was all in a cold sweat. While he spoke, my heart bore witness to the work of God in his; and I felt myself affected as on Whitsunday; was assured it was Christ; said the written Word would bear witness with the personal, and opened it for a sign upon Isa. xlv. 24, 25: 'Surely shall one say, In the Lord have I righteousness and strength: even to Him shall men come, and all that are incensed against Him shall be ashamed. In the Lord shall all the seed of Israel be justified, and shall glory.' I then read, 'Look unto Me, and be ye saved, all the ends of the earth; for I am God, and there is none else. I have sworn by Myself, the word is gone out of My mouth in righteousness, and shall not return, that unto Me every knee shall bow, every tongue shall swear.' And then, 1 Pet. i. 3, 'Blessed be the God and Father of our Lord Jesus Christ, which, according to His abundant mercy, hath begotten us again unto a lively hope, by the resurrection of Jesus Christ from the dead, to an inheritance incorruptible, undefined, and that fadeth not away, reserved in heaven for you, who are kept by the power of God through faith unto salvation.' After this he grew visibly in the faith, and we rejoiced and gave God thanks for the consolation. He appeared a very child; owned he feared nothing so much as offending his Father; was ready to die that moment. In the beginning of prayer he could hardly persuade himself to kneel down, not thinking *he* could find any benefit; so poor, so sinful a creature, what should he pray for?

Returning home in triumph, I found Dr. Byrom; and, in defiance of the tempter, simply told him the great things Jesus had done for me and many others. This drew on a full explanation of the doctrine of faith, which he received with wonderful readiness. Toward midnight I slept in peace.

Thursday, June 8. I had the satisfaction of hearing Mr. Sparks confess himself convinced now that he is under the law, not under grace. In public prayer it pleased the Lord to melt me into humility and love.

At three I took coach for Blendon, with Mr. Bray; and had much talk with a lady about the fall, and faith in Christ. She openly maintained the merit of good works. I would all who oppose the righteousness of faith were so ingenuous; then would they no longer seek it as it were by the works of the law.

Before seven we came to Eltham. In riding thence to Blendon. I was full of delight, and seemed in new heavens and a new earth. We prayed, and sang, and shouted all the way. We found Miss Betsy and Hetty at home, and prayed that this day salvation might come to this house. In the lesson were those words, This is the accepted time, this is the day of salvation.

Friday, June 9. I prayed with fervour for the family. The second lesson was blind Bartimeus. In riding to Bexley with Mr. Piers, I spake of my experience in simplicity and confidence, and found him very ready to receive the faith. We spent the day in the same manner, Mr. Bray relating the inward workings of God upon his soul, and the great things He had lately done for me and our friends at London. He listened eagerly to all that was said, not making the least objection, but confessing it was what he had never experienced. We walked, and sang, and prayed in the garden. He was greatly moved, and testified his full conviction, and desire of finding Christ. 'But I must first,' said he, 'prepare myself by long exercise of prayer and good works.'

At night we joined in prayer for Hetty. Never did I pray with greater earnestness, expecting an immediate answer; and being much disappointed at not finding it, I consulted the Scripture, and met with Jehu's words to his men, 'Let none escape out of your hands.' Then, 'I trust that I shall come shortly.' Still I was in great heaviness for her, and could not sleep till morning. Waking full of desire for her conversion, those words were brought to my remembrance, 'The Spirit and the bride say, Come; and let him that heareth say. Come; and let him that is athirst come: and whosoever will, let him take of the water of life freely.' At this instant came a flash of lightning, then thunder, then violent rain. I accepted it as a sign that the skies would soon pour down righteousness.

Yesterday (the devil of secrecy being expelled) Miss Betsy plainly informed me that, after her last receiving the sacrament, she had heard a voice, 'Go thy way, thy sins are forgiven thee,' and was filled thereby with joy unspeakable. She said within herself, 'Now I do indeed feed upon Christ in my heart by faith,' and continued all day in the spirit of triumph and exultation. All her life, she thought, would be too little to thank God for that day. Yet even after this it was that the enemy got so great advantage over her, in making her oppose the truth with such fierceness. For many days she did not know that she had in herself demonstration of that she denied. But after we had prayed that God would clear up His own work, the darkness of faith dispersed, and those fears that her conversion was not real, by little and little, were all done away.

Saturday, June 10. In the morning lesson was that glorious description of the power of faith: 'Jesus answering said unto them, Have faith in God. For verily I say unto you, That whosoever shall say unto this mountain, Be thou removed, and be thou cast into the sea; and shall not doubt in his heart, but shall believe that those things which he saith shall come to pass; he shall have whatsoever he saith. There fore I say unto you, What things soever ye desire, when ye pray, believe that ye receive them, and ye shall have them.'

We pleaded this promise in behalf of our seeking friends, particularly Hetty and Mr. Piers. He came with his wife. The day before our coming he had been led to read the Homily on Justification, which convinced him that in him dwelt no good thing. Now he likewise saw that the thoughts of his heart were only evil continually, forasmuch as whatsoever is not of faith is sin.

He asked God to give him some comfort, and found it in Luke v. 23, &c.: 'Whether is it easier to say, Thy sins be forgiven thee, or to say, Rise up and walk? But that ye may know that the Son of Man hath power upon earth to forgive sins, (He saith unto the sick of the palsy,) I say unto thee, Arise, and take up thy bed, and go unto thine own house. And immediately he rose up before them, and took up that whereon he lay, and departed to his own house, glorifying God. And they were all amazed, and they glorified God, and were filled with fear, saying, We have seen strange things to-day.'

This was the very miracle, I told him, from which God had shown His intention to heal me; and it was a sign of the like to be done by him. Mr. Bray moved for retiring to prayer. We prayed *after God,* again and again, and asked him, whether he believed Christ could just now manifest Himself to his soul. He answered, 'Yes.' We read him the promise made to the prayer of faith. Mr. Bray bade me speak some promise to him authoritatively, and he should find Christ make it good. I had not faith to do it. He made me pray again, and then read Psalm lxv. I felt every word of it for my friend, particularly, 'Thou that hearest the prayer, unto Thee shall all flesh come. Blessed is the man whom Thou choosest and receivest unto Thee: he shall dwell in Thy court, and shall be satisfied with the plenteousness of Thy house, even of Thy holy temple. Thou shalt show us wonderful things in Thy righteousness, God of our salvation, Thou that art the hope of all the ends of the earth,' &c.

Seeing the great confidence of Mr. Bray, and the deep humility of Mr. Piers, I began to think the promise would be fulfilled before we left the room. My fellow worker with God seemed full of faith and the Holy Ghost, and told him, 'If you can but touch the hem of His garment, you shall be made whole.' We prayed for him a third time, the Spirit greatly helping our infirmities, and then asked if he believed. He answered, 'Yes:' the Spirit witnessing with our spirits, that his heart was as our heart. Bray said, 'I now know of a truth that Christ is in you.' We were all filled with joy; returned thanks, and prayed for a blessing on his ministry; and then brought him down in triumph. Miss Betsy was greatly strengthened hereby, and bold to confess 'she believed.' All her speech now was, 'I only hope that I shall never lose this comfort.'

The day was spent in prayer and conference. Mrs. Piers was, with all ease, convinced of unbelief. After supper I discoursed on faith from the lesson. The poor servants received the word gladly.

Sunday, June 11. While Mr. Piers was preaching upon death, I found great joy in feeling myself willing, or rather desirous, to die. After prayers we joined in intercession for Mr. and Mrs. Delamotte; then for poor Hetty. I received much comfort in reading Luther.

We took coach for church. In singing I observed Hetty join with a mixture of fear and joy. I earnestly prayed, and expected she should meet with something to confirm her in the service. Both the Psalms and lessons were full of consolation.

We adjourned to Mr. Piers, and joined in prayer for a poor woman in despair, one Mrs. Searl, whom Satan had bound these many years. I saw her pass by in the morning, and was touched with a sense of her misery. After pleading His promise of being with us to the end of the world, we went down to her in the name of Jesus. I asked her whether she thought God was love; and not anger, as Satan would persuade her. Then I preached the gospel, which she received with all imaginable eagerness. When we had for some time continued together in prayer, she rose up another creature, strongly and explicitly [declaring] her faith in the blood of Christ, and full persuasion that she was accepted in the Beloved. Hetty then declared that she could not but believe Christ died for her, even for her. We gave thanks for both, with much exultation and triumph.

After family prayer I expounded the lesson, and, going up to my chamber, asked the maid (Mary) how she found herself. She answered, 'Oh, sir, what you said was very comfortable, how that Christ was made sin for me, that I might be made the righteousness of God in Him; that is, He was put in my place, and I in His.' 'Do you then believe this, that Christ died for you?' 'Yes, I do believe it; and I found myself so as I never did before, when you spoke the word.' 'But do you find within yourself that your sins are forgiven?' 'Yes, I do.' These and the like answers, which she made with great simplicity, convinced me that faith had come to her by hearing. We joined in giving glory to God; for we perceived and confessed it was His doing. It pleased Him likewise to bless me with a deep and hitherto unknown dread of ascribing anything to myself.

Monday, June 12. This morning Mrs. Piers told me she had always doubted her having true faith; but now declared with tears, she was convinced her sins were forgiven, and she did believe indeed. We all went to Mrs. Searl, in strong temptation, nothing doubting but we should see the power of Christ triumphing over that of Satan. The enemy had got no advantage over her, though he had laboured all night to trouble and confound her. As often as she named the name of Jesus, he was repelled, and her soul at peace. We were much edified by her deep humility, and preached the gospel to her and her husband, who received it readily. After prayer she rose with 'How shall I be thankful enough to my Saviour?' We parted in a triumphant hymn.

Tuesday, June 13. Mr. Piers was sent for to a dying woman. She was in despair, 'having done so much evil, and so little good.' He declared to her the glad tidings of salvation: that as all her good, were it ten thousand times more, could never save her, so all her evil could never hurt her if she could repent and believe; if she could lay hold on Christ by a living faith, and look for salvation by grace only. This was comfort indeed. She gladly quitted her own merits for Christ's; the Holy Ghost wrought faith in her heart, which she expressed in a calm, cheerful, triumphant expectation of death. Her fears and agonies were at an end. Being justified by faith, she had peace with God; and only entered farther into her rest by dying a few hours after. The spectators were melted into tears. She calmly passed into the heavenly Canaan, and has there brought up a good report of her faithful Pastor, who, under Christ, hath saved her soul from death.

These were the first-fruits of his ministry; and I find him strengthened hereby, and more assured that the gospel is the power of God unto salvation, to every one that believeth. In the evening Mr. Delamotte returned.

Wednesday, June 14. After morning prayer in the little chapel, I kept Hannah from going, that we might first pray for her; but we quickly found there was greater cause of thanksgiving. She told me she was reading a collect last night, which gave her vast pleasure: 'Almighty God, whom truly to know is eternal life, grant us perfectly to know Thy Son Jesus Christ, to be the way, the truth, and the life.' 'To be sure, sir,' said she, 'I found myself so easy immediately, that I cannot tell you.' A few questions fully satisfied us that she was a true believer. Poor Hetty was tempted to imagine she did not believe, because she had not been affected exactly in the same manner with others. We used a prayer for her, and parted.

On the road I overtook Frank, and asked what he thought of these things. He answered, 'I was greatly delighted with one thing you said, how that Christ was made sin for us, that we might be made the righteousness of God in Him.' Upon farther examination I found him manifestly in the faith. We talked and rejoiced together, till we came to Eltham. He there left me, resolved to publish everywhere what things Jesus had done for him.

The coach was filled with young ladies. I was forced to leave off reading, that I might interrupt their scandal. At London I was informed that my brother was gone with Mr. Ingham and Tilchig, to Hernhuth. The news surprised but did not disquiet me.

Thursday, June 15. I was sent for to baptize a child. It gave me occasion to speak upon faith. One of the company was full of self-righteousness. The rest were more patient of the truth, being only gross sinners.

Friday, June 16. After dinner Jack Delamotte came for me. We took coach; and by the way he told me that when we were last together at Blendon, in singing,

Who for me, for me hast died,

he found the words sink into his soul; could have sung for ever, being full of delight and joy: since then has thought himself led, as it were, in every thing; feared nothing so much as offending God; could pray with life; and, in a word, found that he did indeed believe in the Lord Jesus.

I was in the coach with Miss Delamotte. While it stopped I got out to reprove a man for swearing. He thanked me most heartily. We took up Hetty at Blendon, and went on to Bexley.

The next day (Saturday, June 17), we saw, and prayed with, Mrs. Searl, to our mutual encouragement. Mr. Searl heard us gladly. The after noon we passed with our friends at Blendon. Here I was stopped by the return of my pain, and forced to bed. Desires of death continually rose in me, which I laboured to check, not daring to form any wish concerning it.

Sunday, June 18. The pain abated, and the next day left me.

Wednesday, June 21. I was concerned at having been here several days, and done nothing. I preached forgiveness to Mr. Piers's man, who seemed well disposed for receiving it, by a true simplicity. We prayed together, and went to public prayers. In the second lesson was the paralytic healed. I came home with the Miss Delamottes, Mrs. Searl, and the man, who declared before us all that God had given him faith by hearing the sick of the palsy healed. We returned hearty thanks.

The Lord gave us more matter for thanksgiving at Blendon, where I read my brother's sermon on faith. When it was over, the gardener declared faith had come to him by hearing it, and he had no doubt of his sins being forgiven. 'Nay, was I to die just now,' he added, 'I know I should be accepted through Christ Jesus.'

Thursday, June 22. I comforted Hetty, under a strong temptation, because she was not in all points affected like other believers, especially the poor; who have generally a much larger degree of confidence than the rich and learned. I had a proof of this to-day at Mr. Searl's, where, meeting a poor woman, and convincing her of unbelief, I used a prayer for her, that God, who hath chosen the poor of this world to be rich in faith, would now impart to her His unspeakable gift. In the midst of the prayer she received it; avowed it openly, and increased visibly therein.

In the evening we had a meeting at Mr. Piers's, and read my brother's sermon. God set His seal to the truth of it by sending His Spirit upon Mr. Searl and a maid-servant, purifying their hearts by faith. This occasioned our triumphing in the name of Jesus our God.

Friday, June 23. I attended Mr. Piers to a poor old woman, whom he never could prevail upon to go to church. I expected we should be called to preach the law; but found her ready for the gospel, and glad to exchange her merits for Christ's. The evening we passed among our little flock, and parted full of comfort, and peace, and joy.

Saturday, June 24. Riding to Blendon in the morning, I met William Delamotte, just come from Cambridge. He had left town well disposed to the obedience of faith; but now I observed his countenance altered. He had been strongly prejudiced by the good folk at London. At Blendon I found Mr. Delamotte, not over-cordial, yet civil; met letters from my mother, heavily complaining of my brother's forsaking her, and requiring me to accept of the first preferment that offered, on pain of disobedience. This a little disquieted me. I was not much comforted by William Delamotte; but extremely moved for him, and could not refrain from tears. His sisters joined us. I began preaching faith and free grace. His objection was, that it was unjust in God to make sinners equal with us, who had laboured perhaps many years. We proposed singing an hymn. He saw the title, 'Faith in Christ,' and owned he could not bear it.

In our way to church, I again proclaimed to him the glad tidings of salvation. He was exceeding heavy, and, by his own confession, miserable; yet could he not receive this saying, 'We are justified freely by faith alone.' The lesson comforted me concerning him. 'Behold, I will send my messenger, and he shall prepare the way before me: and the Lord, whom ye seek, shall suddenly come to His temple, even the messenger of the covenant, whom ye delight in: behold, He shall come, saith the Lord.' To all such as think it hard to lose the merit of their good works, the Scripture spake as follows: 'Your words have been stout against Me, saith the Lord: yet ye say, What have we spoken so much against thee? Ye have said, It is vain to serve God: and what profit is it that we have kept His ordinances, and that we have walked mournfully before the Lord of hosts?'

Sunday, June 25. I stayed to preach faith to Mrs. Delamotte, whom Providence brought home yesterday, I trust, for that very purpose. I was so faint and full of pain that I had not power to speak: but I had no sooner begun my sermon than all my weakness vanished. God gave me strength and boldness: and after an hour's speaking, I found myself perfectly well. I went and accosted Mrs. Delamotte in her pew: just as shy as I expected. Let it work: God look to the event!

After evening prayer, she just spake to me: Betsy wondered she could bring herself to it. My sermon (I heard) occasioned much disturbance to more than her. Mrs. Searl at night was full of triumph.

Monday, June 26. I waited upon Mrs. Delamotte, expecting what happened. She fell abruptly upon my sermon, for the false doctrine therein. I answered, 'I staked my all upon the truth of it.' She went on, 'It is hard people must have their children seduced in their absence. If every one must have your faith, what will become of all the world? Have you this assurance, Mr. Piers?' 'Yes, madam, in some degree: I thank God for it.' 'I am sorry to hear it.' One of the company cried, 'I am glad to hear it, and bless God for him, and wish all mankind had it too.'

She moved for reading a sermon of Archbishop Sharp's. Piers read. We excepted continually to his unscriptural doctrine. Much dispute ensued. She accused my brother with preaching an instantaneous faith. 'As to that,' I replied, 'we cannot but speak the things which we have seen and heard. I received it in that manner; as have above thirty others in my presence. She started up, said she could not bear it, and ran out of the house. William protested against her behaviour. In the beginning, I had found the old man rise; but I grew calmer and calmer, the longer we talked. Glory be to God through Christ! I offered to go, but they would not let me. Betsy went, and at last prevailed upon her to come in. Nothing more was said. At six I took my leave.

Poor Hannah and Mary came to the door, and caught hold of my hand. Hannah cried, 'Don't be discouraged, sir; I hope we shall all continue steadfast.' I could not refrain from tears. Hetty came in: I exhorted her to persevere. I took horse. William seemed much better disposed than his mother; promised to come and see me the next day. I joined with Mr. Piers in singing,

> Shall I, for fear of feeble man,
> Thy Spirit's course in me restrain?

and in hearty prayer for Mrs. Delamotte.

Tuesday, June 27. Calling upon poor Goody Dickenson, I asked, if she had now forgiveness. 'Yes,' said she, 'I received it in the midst of your sermon.' 'Do you then believe Christ died for you in particular?' 'Yes, to be sure: I must believe it, if I would not deny the Scripture.' She expressed strong confidence in God; appeared full of love to two beggars that called; believed she should be saved, if she died just now; would come to church, if all in rags. In short, she left me no reason to doubt but that she was taken in at the eleventh hour, being now near fourscore.

Coming back to Mr. Piers's, I found W. Delamotte. I was full of hope for him. He told me he had wrote two sheets against the truth; but in seeking after more texts, had met one that quite spoiled all. 'Not by works of righteousness which we have done, but according to His mercy He saved us.' This convinced him; and immediately he burnt all he had wrote. I asked what it was he still stuck at. 'Nothing,' said he, 'but God's giving faith instantaneously.' I replied, that alone hindered his receiving it just now; no more preparation being absolutely necessary thereto than what God is pleased to give.

We were directed to many apposite Scriptures, particularly Luke vii. 47: 'Wherefore I say unto thee, Her sins, which are many, are forgiven.' John xx. 27, 28: 'Then said He to Thomas, Reach hither thy finger, and behold My hands; and reach hither thy hand, and thrust it into My side: and be not faithless, but believing. And Thomas answered and said unto Him, My Lord and my God.'

We went to prayers, pleaded the promises for him with great earnestness and tears: then read 2 Thess. i. 11, 12: 'Wherefore also we pray always for you, that our God would count you worthy of this calling, and fulfil all the good pleasure of His goodness, and the work of faith with power: that the name of our Lord Jesus Christ may be glorified in you, and ye in Him, according to the grace of our God and the Lord Jesus Christ.' I observed the workings of God strong upon him, and prayed again. Then read the scriptures that first offered: Titus iii. 5: 'Not by works of righteousness which we have done,' &c. (The very text that stopped him in the morning.) Amos iv. 12: 'Because I will do this to thee, prepare to meet thy God.' Psalm lxviii. 6: 'God setteth the solitary in families, He bringeth out those which are bound with chains:' and lastly, Ps. lxvi. 20: 'Blessed be God, which hath not turned away my prayer, nor His mercy from me.'

While we were praying, and singing, and reading, alternately, a poor man, one Mr. Heather, came to talk with me. He had heard and liked the sermon upon faith. I asked him whether he had faith. 'No.' Whether forgiveness of sins. No. Whether there was or could be any good in him till he believed. 'No.' But do you think Christ cannot give you faith and forgiveness in this hour? 'Yes, to be sure He can.' 'And do you believe His promise, that when two of His disciples shall agree upon earth, as touching anything they shall ask of Him, He will give it them?' 'I do.' 'Why, then, here is your minister, and I agree to ask faith for you.' 'Then I believe I shall receive it before I go out of the room.'

We went to prayer directly; pleaded the promise; and rising, asked him whether he believed. His answer was, 'Yes, I do believe with all my heart. I believe Christ died for my sins. I know they are all forgiven. I desire only to love Him. I would suffer anything for Him: could lay down my life for Him this moment.' I turned to my scholar, and said, 'Do you now believe that God can give faith instantaneously?' He was too full to speak; but told me afterwards he envied the unopposing ignorance and simplicity of the poor, and wished himself that illiterate carpenter.

Next day I returned to town, rejoicing that God had added to His living church seven more souls through my ministry. 'Not unto me, O Lord, not unto me, but to Thy name be the praise, for Thy loving-mercy, and for Thy truth's sake.' I had hopes of seeing greater things than these, from a scripture He this day directed me to: Luke v. 9: 'For he was astonished, and all that were with him, at the draught of fishes which they had taken.'

I went to Mr. Sims's, in expectation of Christ. Several of our friends were providentially brought thither. We joined in singing and prayer. The last time we prayed, I could not leave off, but was still forced to go on. I rose at last, and saw Mr. Chapman still kneeling. I opened the Book, and read aloud, 'And, behold, a woman, which was diseased with an issue of blood twelve years, came behind Him, and touched the hem of His garment: for she said within herself, If I may but touch His garment, I shall be whole. And Jesus turned Him about, and when He saw her, He said, Daughter, be of good comfort; thy faith hath made thee whole. And the woman was made whole from that hour.' My heart burned within me while I was reading: at the same time I heard him cry out, with great struggling, 'I do believe.' We lifted him up; for he had not power to rise of himself, being quite helpless, exhausted, and in a profuse sweat. An old believer among us owned himself affected with a wonderful sympathy. We had the satisfaction of *seeing* Mr. Chapman increase in faith; and returned most hearty thanks to the God of his and our salvation.

Thursday, June 29. Miss Suky Claggett called, and to my no small comfort informed me of her sister's lately receiving faith. She likewise brought me an invitation from her mother. Mrs. Turner would have sent for her (Miss B. Claggett), but I would not suffer it; that I might have no hand at all in the matter. I sat down to write; when Miss Betsy came for me. We joined in thanksgiving for her, and intercession for her mother; and then took coach. Mrs. Turner made the fourth.

I sought to the oracle for direction, and was much strengthened by the answer, from Acts x. 29: 'Therefore came I unto you without gainsaying, as soon as I was sent for: I ask therefore for what intent ye have sent for me?' What makes it more remarkable is, that it is St. Peter's day. We all conceived great hopes of Mrs. Claggett. I found her very courteous, well-disposed, emptied of herself. We sang, and at her desire prayed together. She freely confessed how greatly she had been prejudiced against the truth; but was thoroughly satisfied by my reading the sermon. I prayed after it, without much affection; again with more; and the third time strongly moved. I *knew* that she believed. I believed for her. The Scripture gave the strongest testimony of it. At first she said she must not presume to say she believed; but grew more and more confirmed. I left her, in confidence God would soon clear up His own work in her soul, beyond all doubt or contradiction. Soon after, to keep me from being lifted up, the messenger of Satan was suffered to buffet me.

Friday, June 30. Thanks be to God, the first thing I felt to-day was a fear of pride, and desire of love. Betsy Delamotte called, and gave me the following letter:

Dear Sir, God hath heard your prayers. Yesterday, about twelve, He put His *fiat* to the desires of His distressed servant; and, glory be to Him, I have enjoyed the fruits of His Holy Spirit ever since. The only uneasiness I feel is want of thankfulness and love for so unspeakable a gift. But I am confident of this also, that the same gracious Hand which hath communicated will communicate even unto the end.

I am your sincere friend in Christ,

W. DELAMOTTE.

'O my friend, I am free indeed! I agonized some time betwixt darkness and light; but God was greater than my heart, and burst the cloud, and broke down the partition-wall, and opened to me the door of faith.'

In reading this, I felt true thankfulness, and was quite melted down with God's goodness to my friend.

I followed His guidance in the afternoon to Mr. Sims's. We spent the time as usual. Mrs. Chapman called; said she could not stay; yet stayed prayers. I was much assisted; rose, and asked her whether she believed. 'I do not know but I do; for I never found myself so in my life; so strangely warmed! I seem to have a fire within me. I thought, while kneeling down, "How could I expect to receive faith, when so many better than I were here?" It then came into my mind, that I had left my money upon the stall; but God, thought I, could take care of it, or give me a better thing.' We concluded the day with prayer at Mr. Bray's.

Saturday, July 1. I was again at Mrs. Claggett's. The eldest daughter and Mrs. Claggett joined us. I related the cure of the lame girl at Bath. She rejoiced

91

to hear a person might have faith, and have it long obscured by worldly cares, yet not lost: said the maid's case was hers; professed her now believing, and owned the darkness she had long lain under a just punishment for her not giving God the glory. We sang, and rejoiced together, and went to the house of God as friends. In the lesson He related His past kindness to her. 'And He was teaching in one of the synagogues on the Sabbath day. And, behold, there was a woman which had a spirit of infirmity eighteen years, and was bowed together, and could in no wise lift up herself. And when Jesus saw her, He called her to Him, and said unto her, Woman, thou art loosed from thine infirmity. And He laid His hands on her: and immediately she was made straight, and glorified God.' Mrs. Claggett was deeply affected; and told me after wards, that her not following the woman's example of glorifying God had occasioned all the troubles of her life: but she was now resolved, as far as in her lay, to repair her past unfaithfulness .

At Mr. Sims's I was extremely averse to prayer; would fain have stole away without it: but Mr. Bray stopped me, saying my deadness could not hinder God, and forced me to pray. I had scarce begun, when I was quite melted down, and prayed more fervently than ever before. A poor man, who came in at the beginning of the prayer, now confessed his faith before us all, being full of joy and triumph. 'He never found himself so before; knew his sins were forgiven; could gladly die that moment.'

Sunday, July 2. Being to preach this morning for the first time, I received strength for the work of the ministry, in prayer and singing. The whole service at Basingshaw was wonderfully animating, especially the Gospel concerning the miraculous draught of fishes. I preached salvation by faith to a deeply attentive audience; I gave the cup. Observing a woman full of reverence, I asked her if she had forgiveness of sins. She answered, with great sweetness and humility, 'Yes, I know it now that I have forgiveness.'

I preached again at London Wall, without fear or weariness. As I was going into the church, a woman caught hold of my hand, and blessed me most heartily, telling me she had received forgiveness of sins while I was preaching in the morning.

In the evening we met, a troop of us, at Mr. Sims's. There was one Mrs. Harper there, who had this day in like manner received the Spirit, by the hearing of faith; but feared to confess it. We sung the hymn to Christ. At the words,

Who for me, for me hath died,

she burst out into tears and outcries, 'I believe, I believe!' and sunk down. She continued, and increased in the assurance of faith; full of peace, and joy, and love.

We sang and prayed again. I observed one of the maids run out, and, following, found her full of tears, and joy, and love. I asked what ailed her. She answered, as soon as joy would let her, that 'Christ died for her!' She appeared quite overpowered with His love.

Monday, July 3. I had some discourse with my friendly namesake, Charles Rivington. I begged him to suspend his judgement till he heard me preach.

Tuesday, July 4. I received a letter from my brother at Tiverton, full of heavy charges. At Mr. Sparks's I found Jephtha Harris. I convinced him so far, that he owned he had been prejudiced against the truth, and had not faith. I carried him to Mr. Bray's; prayed over him, and pleaded the promises. All were much affected.

I corrected a sermon of Mr. Sparks's on justification. Took coach for Bexley. In the way I was enabled to pray for my brother. I heard a good account of Mrs. Delamotte, that she was almost beat out of her own righteousness.

Honest Frank made one of our congregation this evening, and gave a comfortable account of the little flock at Blendon. I received a fuller from Hetty; informing me that her mother was convinced of unbelief, and much ashamed of her behaviour towards me.

Wednesday, July 5. William Delamotte came, and rejoiced with me for all God had done. We brought a woman home from church, and laboured hard to convince her she deserved hell. Another confessed her having received forgiveness of sins in sickness.

Friday, July 7. Mrs. Delamotte followed me from church, sent for me down, hoped she did not interrupt me. Her third sentence was, 'Well, Mr. Wesley, are you still angry with me?' 'No, Madam,' I answered, 'nor ever was. Before I gave myself time to consider, I was myself so violent against the truth, that I know to make allowance for others.' Here we came to a full explanation; produced the scriptures which prove our justification by faith only, the witness of the Spirit, &c. By these, and an excellent sermon of Bishop Beveridge's on the subject, she seemed thoroughly convinced. All she stuck at was the instantaneousness of faith, or, in other words, the possibility of any one's perceiving when the life of faith first began.

She carried me in her coach to Blendon, where the poor servants were overjoyed to see me once more. While we were praying for her, she sent for me up to her closet. I found her quite melted into an humble, contrite, longing frame of spirit. She showed me several prayers attesting the true faith, especially that of Bishop Taylor: 'I know, O blessed Jesus, that Thou didst take upon Thee my nature, that Thou mightest suffer for my sins; that Thou didst suffer to deliver me from them, and from Thy Father's wrath. And I was delivered from His wrath, that I might serve Thee, in holiness and righteousness all my days. Lord, I am as sure Thou didst the great work of redemption for me, and for all mankind, as that I am alive. This is my hope, the strength of my spirit, my joy, and my confidence. And do Thou never let the spirit of unbelief enter into me, and take me from this rock. Here I will dwell; for I have a delight therein. Here I will live, and here I desire to die.'

She asked me what she could do more, being convinced of her want of faith, and not able to give it herself. I preached the freeness of the grace, and betook myself to prayer for her, labouring, sighing, looking for the witness of the Spirit, the fullness of the promises, in her behalf. I conjured her to expect continually the accomplishment of the promise, and not think her confessed unworthiness any bar. Next morning I returned to town.

Sunday, July 9. I preached my brother's sermon upon faith at ___, and a second time in St. Sepulchre's vestry. In walking home with Mrs. Burton, I said, 'Surely there must be something which you are not willing to give up, or God would have given you comfort before now.' She answered only by her tears. After praying for her at Mr. Bray's, I lay down; rose; stopped her going home, and carried her with James and Mrs. Turner from the company to pray. After prayer, in which I was much assisted, I found her under a great concern, trembling, and cold; longing, yet dreading, to say 'she believed.' We prayed again. She then said, with much struggling, 'Lord, I believe; help Thou my unbelief.' She repeated it several times, and gained strength by each repetition.

Monday, July 10. At Mr. Sparks's request, I went with him, Mr. Bray, and Mr. Burnham, to Newgate; and preached to the ten male factors under sentence of death; but with a heavy heart. My old prejudices against the possibility of a death-bed repentance still hung upon me; and I could hardly hope there was mercy for those whose time was so short. But in the midst of my languid discourse, a sudden spirit of faith came upon me, and I promised them all pardon, in the name of Jesus Christ, if they would then, as at the last hour, repent, and believe the gospel. Nay, I did believe they would accept of the proffered mercy, and could not help telling them, 'I had no doubt but God would give me every soul of them.'

In going to Mr. Chapman's I met Margaret Beutiman, and bade her follow, for we were several of us to join in prayer there. James Hutton, Mr. Holland, Mr. and Mrs. Sims got thither soon after us. We sang, and pleaded the promises. In the midst of prayer, Margaret received the atonement, and professed her faith without wavering; her love to Christ, and willingness to die that moment. We returned thanks for her, and I then offered to go. They pressed me to stay a little longer: I did so, and heard Mrs. Storer, a sister of Mr. Bray's, complain of the hardness of her heart. She owned she had been under the utmost uneasiness since our last meeting at her brother's, unable to pray, or find any rest to her soul. While we were singing the hymn to the Father, she did find the rest she sighed after; was quite pierced, as she said, her heart ready to burst, and her whole nature overpowered. We went to prayers, and then opened the Scripture, 'I thank Thee, O Father, Lord of heaven and earth, that Thou hast hid these things from the wise and prudent, and hast revealed them unto babes.' She then was strengthened to profess her faith, and increased in peace and joy. As we walked, she said she could not have conceived how these things could be; what the change was which we spoke of. Her faith was farther confirmed by public prayer; and she continued all the evening full of comfort, and peace that passeth all understanding.

Tuesday, July 11. I preached with earnestness to the prisoners from the second lesson. One or two of them were deeply affected. At Bray's I found a letter from W. Delamotte, and read, with joy and thankfulness, as follows:

'I cannot keep pace: the mercies of God come in so abundantly on our unworthy family, that I am not able to declare them. Yet, as they are His blessings through your ministry, I must inform you of them, as they will strengthen your hands, and prove helpers of your joy.

'Great, then, I believe, was the struggle between nature and grace in the soul of my mother; but God, who knoweth the very heart and reins, hath searched her out. Her spirit, like Naaman's flesh, is returned as that of a little child. She is converted, and Christ hath spoken peace to her soul. This work was begun in her the morning you left us, though she concealed it from you.

'When she waked, the following scripture was strongly suggested to her: "Either what woman, having ten pieces of silver, if she lose one, doth not light a candle, and sweep the house, and seek diligently till she find it." She rose immediately, took up Bishop Taylor, and opened upon a place which so strongly asserted this living faith, that she was fully convinced. But the enemy preached humility to her; that she could not deserve so great a gift. However, God still pursued, and she could not long forbear communicating the emotion of her soul to me. We prayed, read, and conversed for an hour; the Lord made use of a mean instrument to convince her of her ignorance in the Word. Throughout that day her mind was more and more enlightened, till at length she broke out, "Where have I been? I know nothing; I see nothing. My mind is all darkness. How have I opposed the Scripture!" The tempter, thus enraged, excited all his powers to persuade her she was labouring after something that was not to be attained; but Christ suffered her not to fall. She flew to Him in prayer and singing; and though Satan damped her much, yet could he not conquer her, because that which was conceived in her was of the Holy Ghost.

'She continued agonizing all the evening. But how can I utter the sequel? The first object of her thoughts the next morning was Christ. She saw Him approaching; and seeing, loved, believed, adored. Her prayers drew Him still nearer; and everything she saw concurred to hasten the embrace of her Beloved. Thus she continued in the Spirit till four; when, reading in her closet, she received the kiss of reconciliation. Her own soul could not contain the joys attending it. She could not forbear imparting to her friends and neighbours that she had found the piece which she had lost. Satan in vain at tempted to shake her; for she felt in herself,

> Faith's assurance, hope's increase,
> All the confidence of love.

Mr. Sparks this morning asked me whether I would preach for him at St. Helen's. I agreed to supply Mr. Broughton's place, who is now at Oxford, arming our friends against the faith. The pain in my side was very violent; but I looked up to Christ, and owned His healing power. At the same time, that came into my mind, Out of weakness were made strong. No sooner did I enter the coach than the pain left me, and I preached faith in Christ to a vast congregation with great boldness, adding much extempore.

After sermon, Mrs. Hind, with whom Mr. Broughton lodges, sent for me; owned her agreement to the doctrine, and pressed me to come and talk with Mr. Broughton, who, she could not but believe, must himself agree to it.

From her I went to Mr. Sims, and found that God had set His seal to my ministry; Mr. Dandy and Miss Branford declaring faith had come to them by hearing me. We rejoiced, and gave thanks from the ground of the heart.

Wednesday, July 12. I preached at Newgate to the condemned felons, and visited one of them in his cell, sick of a fever - a poor black that had robbed his master. I told him of One who came down from heaven to save lost sinners, and him in particular; described the sufferings of the Son of God, His sorrows, agony, and death. He listened with all the signs of eager astonishment; the tears trickled down his cheeks while he cried, 'What! was it for me? Did God suffer all this for so poor a creature as me?' I left him waiting for the salvation of God.

In the evening Mr. Washington of Queen's came to dispute with me. I simply testified my want of faith three months ago, and my having it now; asked whether he could lay down his life for the truth of his being in the faith; whether he allowed Christ to be as really present in the believing soul as in the third heavens; told him he was yet in his sins, and knew nothing, and begged him to pray for direction.

Thursday, July 13. I read prayers and preached at Newgate, and administered the sacrament to our friends, with five of the felons. I was much affected and assisted in prayer for them; and exhorted them with great comfort and confidence.

Friday, July 14. I received the sacrament from the Ordinary; spake strongly to the poor malefactors; and to the sick negro in the condemned hole, moved by his sorrow and earnest desire of Christ Jesus.

Saturday, July 15. I preached there again with an enlarged heart; and rejoiced with my poor happy black; who now *believes* the Son of God loved him, and gave Himself for him.

Sunday, July 16. Metcalf and Savage came: the latter received faith on Friday night, in prayer, and is now filled with comfort, peace, and joy. I took coach with Metcalf; preached the threefold state with boldness; gave the sacrament. I went thence to Mrs. Claggett's; sang, rejoiced, and gave thanks, in behalf of both the maids, now added to the church by true divine faith. Mr. Claggett coming in by mistake, we laid hold on and carried him with us to Blackfriars. Very weak and faint, yet was I strengthened to preach for above an hour. I was carried to bed full of pain, expecting my fever; yet believing it could not return, unless it were best.

Monday, July 17. I rose free from pain. At Newgate I preached on death (which they must suffer the day after to-morrow). Mr. Sparks assisted in giving the sacrament. Another clergyman was there. Newington asked me to go in the coach with him. At one I was with the black in his cell, James Hutton assisting. Two more of the malefactors came. I had great help and power in prayer. One rose, and said, he felt his heart all on fire, so as he never found himself before; he was all in a sweat; believed Christ died for him. I found myself overwhelmed with the love of Christ to sinners. The black was quite happy. The other criminal was in an excellent temper; believing, or on the point of it. I talked with another, concerning faith in Christ: he was greatly moved. The Lord, I trust, will help *his* unbelief also.

I joined at Bray's with Hutton, Holland, Burton, in fervent prayer and thanksgiving. At six I carried Bray and Fish to Newgate again, and talked chiefly with Hudson and Newington. N. declared he had felt, some time ago in prayer, inexpressible joy and love; but was much troubled at its being so soon withdrawn. The Lord gave power to pray. They were deeply affected. We have great hopes of both.

Tuesday, July 18. The Ordinary read prayers and preached. I administered the sacrament to the black, and eight more; having first instructed them in the nature of it. I spake comfortably to them afterwards.

In the cells, one told me that whenever he offered to pray, or had a serious thought, something came and hindered him; was with him almost continual-ly; and once appeared. After we had prayed for him *in faith,* he rose amazing-ly comforted, full of joy and love; so that we could not doubt his having re-ceived the atonement.

At night I was locked in with Bray in one of the cells. We wrestled in mighty prayer. All the criminals were present, and all delightfully cheerful. The soldier, in particular, found his comfort and joy increase every moment. An other, from the time he communicated, has been in perfect peace. Joy was visible in all their faces. We sang:

> Behold the Saviour of mankind,
>   Nailed to the shameful tree!
> How vast the love that Him inclined
>   To bleed and die for thee, &c.

It was one of the most triumphant hours I have ever known. Yet on

Wednesday, July 19, I rose very heavy, and backward to visit them for the last time. At six I prayed and sang with them all together. The Ordinary would read prayers, and preached most miserably. Mr. Sparks and Mr. Broughton were present. I felt my heart full of tender love to the latter. He administered. All the ten received. Then he prayed; and I after him.

At half-hour past nine their irons were knocked off, and their hands tied. I went in a coach with Sparks, Washington, and a friend of Newington's (N. himself not being permitted). By half-hour past ten we came to Tyburn, wait-ed till eleven: then were brought the children appointed to die. I got upon the cart with Sparks and Broughton: the Ordinary endeavoured to follow, when the poor prisoners begged he might not come; and the mob kept him down.

I prayed first, then Sparks and Broughton. We had prayed before that our Lord would show there was a power superior to the fear of death. Newington had quite forgot his pain. They were all cheerful; full of comfort, peace, and triumph; assuredly persuaded Christ had died for them, and waited to receive them into paradise. Greenaway was impatient to be with Christ.

The black had spied me coming out of the coach, and saluted me with his looks. As often as his eyes met mine, he smiled with the most composed, delightful countenance I ever saw. Read caught hold of my hand in a transport of joy. Newington seemed perfectly pleased. Hudson declared he was never better, or more at ease, in mind and body. None showed any natural terror of death: no fear, or crying, or tears. All expressed their desire of our following them to paradise. I never saw such calm triumph, such incredible indifference to dying. We sang several hymns; particularly,

> Behold the Saviour of mankind,
> Nailed to the shameful tree;

and the hymn entitled, Faith in Christ, which concludes,

> A guilty, weak, and helpless worm,
> Into Thy hands I fall:
> Be Thou my life, my righteousness,
> My Jesus, and my all.

We prayed Him, in earnest faith, to receive their spirits. I could do nothing but rejoice: kissed Newington and Hudson; took leave of each in particular. Mr. Broughton bade them not be surprised when the cart should draw away. They cheerfully replied, they should not; expressed some concern how we should get back to our coach. We left them going to meet their Lord, ready for the Bridegroom. When the cart drew off, not one stirred, or struggled for life, but meekly gave up their spirits. Exactly at twelve they were turned off. I spoke a few suitable words to the crowd; and returned, full of peace and confidence in our friends' happiness. That hour under the gallows was the most blessed hour of my life.

At Mr. Bray's we renewed our triumph. I found my brother and sister Lambert there, and preached to them the gospel of forgiveness, which they received without opposition.

Thursday, July 20. At morning prayers in Islington. I had some serious conversation with Mr. Stonehouse, the Vicar. I brought him home with me from evening prayers.

Friday, July 21. Mr. Robson came; and received the strange doctrine of faith with surprising readiness. At night many joined us in prayer and praise. Brother Edmunds bore his testimony; so did two others, who had received the blessing of pardon, in hearing my sermon upon 'The voice of one crying in the wilderness, Prepare ye the way of the Lord.' Another stood up (lately a notorious sinner), and declared the same. We continued till eleven, praying, and praising God.

Saturday, July 22. Mr. Robson confessed he did believe there was such a faith, but it was impossible for him to obtain it; and it must necessarily bring on a persecution. We continued pleading the promises for him: he was greatly moved, and grew stronger and stronger in hope. I was full of expectation, as well as Mr. Bray. In singing the hymn to the Father, our poor friend was quite overpowered, and even compelled to believe; till at last he was filled with strength and confidence.

At five Mr. Chapman came from Mr. Broughton, and appeared entirely estranged. He insisted that there is no need of our being persecuted now. I told him I .was of a different judgement; and believed every doctrine of God must have these two marks: (1) Meeting all the opposition of men and devils; (2) Triumphing over all. I expressed my readiness to part with him, and all my friends and relations, for the truth's sake; avowed my liberty and happiness since Whit Sunday; made a bridge for a flying enemy, and we parted tolerable friends.

Monday, July 24. I preached faith at Mr. Stonehouse's. Still he stuck upon fitness. We prayed most earnestly. Miss Claggetts dined with us. I prayed again, with great comfort and hope for him. He continued insensible. We bade him open the Bible. He did, on these apposite words: 1 Thess. i. 5, 'For our gospel came not unto you in word only, but also in power, and in the Holy Ghost, and in much assurance.' I stayed with him after evening prayer, to keep him from Mr. Chapman. I agreed to take charge of his parish, under him, as his curate. At night Mrs. Turner told me at Mrs. Claggett's that she had been greatly strengthened to pray in faith for Mr. Stonehouse.

Tuesday, July 25. William Delamotte came, and carried me to Bexley.

Wednesday, July 26. At Blendon. Mrs. Delamotte called upon me to rejoice with her, in the experience of the divine goodness. In the evening I met several sincere seekers at Mr. Piers's, with some who knew in whom they have believed. We had great power in prayer, and joy in thanksgiving. W. Delamotte often shouted for joy. Before nine we got back to Blendon. Mrs. Delamotte then confessed that all her desire had been to affront, or make me angry; that she had long watched every word I said; had persecuted the truth, and all who professed it, &c.

Thursday, July 27. In the coach to London I preached faith in Christ. A lady was extremely offended; avowed her own merits in plain terms; asked if I was not a Methodist; threatened to beat me. I declared I deserved nothing but hell; so did she; and must confess it, before she could have a title to heaven. This was most intolerable to her. The others were less offended; began to listen; asked where I preached: a maid-servant devoured every word.

Friday, July 28. Mr. Exell received faith, in immediate answer to our prayers. At Mr. Stonehouse's I met Charles Rivington and his wife; but could come to no agreement, I insisting on a particular manifestation of Christ to every soul, and he denying it.

Sunday, July 30. At six I received the sacrament; preached faith at ten; and again in the afternoon at All Hallows, Thames Street. My strength increased with my labour. At Mr. Sims's I began expounding the Epistle to the Romans.

Monday, July 31. I began writing a sermon upon Gal. iii. 22: 'But the Scripture hath concluded all under sin, that the promise by faith of Jesus Christ might be given to them that believe.'

I met Mr. Lynn, who had often asked me to his house. I went; and found him again convinced of unbelief, and more uneasy than ever.

Tuesday, August 1. I read prayers at Islington (as I do most days), and slept at Mr. Stonehouse's.

Thursday, August 3. I met Lord Egmont, and declared my intention of returning to Georgia, if my health permitted; with which he was much pleased.

I corrected Mr. Whitefield's Journal for the press; my advice to suppress it being overruled.

Sunday, August 6. I preached at Islington, and gave the cup. In the afternoon I read prayers in a church in London, and preached again. I was faint and full of pain when I began; but my work quite cured me.

Thursday, August 10. I walked to Mrs. Hind's. Mr. Broughton and Washington were there. They denied explicitly that we are saved by Christ's imputed righteousness; and affirmed that works do justify; have a share in making us righteous before God. I appealed to the Homilies, which they had never read, for justification by faith only. When they were gone, I had much lively conversation with Mrs. Hind and her son, well-disposed to receive faith, if they have it not already.

Saturday, August 12. We were warmed by reading George Whitefield's Journal. I walked with Metcalf, &c., in great joy, wishing for a place to sing in, when a blacksmith stopped us. We turned into his house, sang an hymn, and went on our way rejoicing.

Sunday, August 13. I preached at Islington; gave the sacrament to a sick woman, who was therein assured of her reconciliation to God through Christ Jesus.

Tuesday, August 15. I communicated again with the sick woman. Mrs. Claggett and her daughters made the greater part of the congregation. We were all comforted. I seldom fail seeing them and Islington once a day. f

Wednesday, August 16. I was dragged out by Mr. Bray to Jeph. Harris's religious Society; when, after much disputing, I confuted, rather than convinced, them, by reading the Homily on Justification.

Thursday, August 17. I preached faith to a dying woman, and administered the sacrament. She was satisfied God had sent us: told me I was the instrument of saving her soul. I asked, 'Had you then no faith before we came?' She answered, 'No: how should I? it is the gift of God; and He never gave it me till now.' 'Do you now think you shall be saved?' 'Yes,' she replied, smiling; 'I have no doubt of it.' 'You need not then fear the devil's hurting you.' 'I know that; he is chained: I have nothing to do with him, or he with me.' She promised to bring up a good report of us to those she was going to.

I read prayers at Islington; met Mrs. Brockmar one who in despair had been directed to Christ, and in a fortnight found peace to her soul, steadfastly believing her sin had been imputed to Christ, and His righteousness to her. She asked me to go and see the sick woman again. I preached faith to a large company I found there. The woman bore a noble testimony. I asked her before them all, 'Have you received forgiveness?' Her answer was, 'Yes, I am assured of it by Christ Himself.' To them she said, they must not *think* they believe, but *feel* it, and have a full confidence thereof. They all thanked me much.

Friday, August 18. I prayed and rejoiced with her again, yet more ascertained of her salvation. Mrs. Brockmar, the Claggetts, &c., were of the company. We got upon the leads and sang; full of zeal, and life, and comfort. I read prayers; and, with Mr. Brockmar and others, returned to singing at Mr. Stonehouse's. He read us an Homily. At seven we all walked out; were driven by the hard rain to a shed, where we sang and preached to those about us. I came, wet through, to Mr. Bray's; joined our friends there in singing, reading, and prayer. A young man received faith in that hour.

Saturday, August 19. At Mr. Stonehouse's I read prayers with some life. I gave the sacrament to the woman: asked, 'Do you still believe you shall be saved?' 'Yes; I am humbly confident of it, and care not how soon I depart. I desire to be dissolved, and to be with Christ.' We sang on the leads, as before.

At three I found my friend Stonehouse exceeding heavy, and sorely distressed through fear of marrying. I prayed earnestly that neither he nor I might ever be left to follow our own heart's desires. After reading prayers, I buried a corpse: and went back to Bray's, weighed down with my poor George's burden.

Sunday, August 20. I preached at Islington in the morning, at Clerkenwell in the afternoon, on 'The Scripture hath concluded all under sin,' &c. God gave me great boldness; and the Word, I trust, did not return empty.

Monday, August 21. Mr. Stonehouse's maid, Thomasin, told me she had found great peace, and comfort, and joy, in prayer last Saturday, so that her very inside (as she expressed it) was changed. I visited Mrs. Hall, a-dying. She made signs of her confident faith. Then Mrs. Hankinson; who told me she had been very uneasy ever since I said a person must be sure of their forgiveness. I preached faith, as the only instrument of justification. She was quite melted down. We prayed: she rose, and said her heart was set at liberty, her burden taken away, and her spirit joyful in Christ her Saviour.

Thursday, August 24. At Mrs. Musgrave's I met one Mrs. Nichols; who readily owned she was not free, had not faith; but believed Christ could just then give it her. We prayed for her in faith. She received the immediate answer;

expressed her confidence, delight, and love of Jesus; and, at the same time, her utter defiance of Satan, sin, and death.

Saturday, August 26. I was with Mr. Stonehouse: possessed with a strange fancy that a man must be wholly sanctified before he can know that he is justified.

Sunday, August 27. I preached at St. John's the three-fold state, and helped to administer the sacrament to a very large congregation.

Monday, August 28. I came in the coach to Oxford; rejoiced at Mr. Fox's, with Mr. Kinchin, Hutchins, and other Christian friends.

Tuesday, August 29. I preached to the poor prisoners in the Castle. Many, with Mr. Watson, were present at the Society. All of one mind; earnestly seeking Christ. I read the Homilies, and continued instant in prayer. A woman cried out, 'Where have I been so long? I have been in darkness: I shall never be delivered out of it' - and burst into tears. Mrs. Cleminger, too, appeared in the pangs of the new birth.

Wednesday, August 30. I left Mr. Watson convinced of unbelief, and rode to Stanton Harcourt. I spoke with great reluctance, yet fully and plainly, to my sister; and then to Mr. Gambold and Kinchin, who surprised me by receiving my hard saying that they had not faith. I was ashamed to see the great thankfulness, and childlike, loving spirit of Mr. Kinchin, even before justification.

Thursday, August 31. I waited upon the Dean; but we could not quite agree in our notions of faith. He wondered we had not hit upon the Homilies sooner: treated me with great candour and friendliness.

At the Society I read my sermon, 'The Scripture hath concluded all under sin,' and urged upon each my usual question, 'Do you deserve to be damned?' Mrs. Platt, with the utmost vehemence, cried out, 'Yes; I do, I do!' I prayed that if God saw there any contrite soul, He would fulfil His promise of coming and making His abode with it. 'If Thou hast sent Thy Spirit to reprove any sinner of sin, in the name of Jesus Christ, I claim salvation for that sinner!' Again she broke out into strong cries, but of joy, not sorrow, being quite overpowered with the love of Christ. I asked her if she believed in Jesus. She answered in full assurance of faith. We sang and rejoiced over her (she still continued kneeling), joined in thanksgiving; but her voice was heard above ours.

Mr. Kinchin asked, Have you forgiveness of sins? 'I am perfectly assured I have.' 'Have you the earnest of the Spirit in your heart?' 'I have; I know I have: I feel it now within.' Her answers to these and the like questions were expressive of the strongest confidence, to the great encouragement of all present. I related this at Hutchins's, before Mr. Wells, who seems fully convinced of the truth.

Friday, September 1. I took coach for London. Between five and six reached Mrs. Claggett's. They heartily joined me in praise and prayer. Mr. Claggett was very friendly. James Hutton supped with us. I found several at Bray's. After prayer he told me God plainly forbids my return to America, by my success here.

Sunday, September 3. I preached salvation by faith at Westminster Abbey; gave the cup. In the afternoon I preached at St. Botolph's; and expounded Rom. ii., at Sims's, to above two hundred people.

Monday, September 4. Charles Kinchin, now my inseparable companion, accompanied me to Bexley and Blendon. I prayed, and was comforted with the poor people.

Tuesday, September 5. Mr. Piers agreed to board my sister Kezzy. I read my sermon; prayed and rejoiced with Mrs. Delamotte, and the rest at Blendon. Charles was all thankfulness and love. I returned to town very ill of a sore throat.

Sunday, September 10. I preached faith in the morning at Sir George Wheler's chapel, and assisted at the sacrament. In the afternoon at St. Botolph's. In the evening at Sims's I was much strengthened to pray and expound to above three hundred attentive souls. Another lost sheep was now brought home.

Friday, September 15. Meeting Charles Metcalf's mother, I laboured to convince her of unbelief (our first point with all). She yielded at last; and we joined in earnest prayer for her.

Saturday, September 16. James Hutton came, and carried me perforce to Newgate; where we preached Christ to four condemned prisoners. At night my brother returned from Hernhuth. We took sweet counsel together, comparing our experiences.

Sunday, September 17. At the early sacrament my brother read prayers; I preached all under sin in Gracechurch Street, the morning; at Queen's Street chapel in the afternoon. In the evening I preached faith, from Rom. iii., at the Savoy Society. My brother entertained us at night with the Moravian experiences.

Friday, September 22. At Bray's I expounded Eph. i. A dispute arising about absolute predestination, I entered my protest against that doctrine.

Sunday, September 24. I comforted Mrs. Claggett, much threatened by her husband; and then Mrs. Hankinson, who has lost several boarders, yet is in nothing terrified by her adversaries. I read prayers in Islington church, and preached with great boldness. There was a vast audience, and better disposed than usual. None went out, as they had threatened, and frequently done heretofore; especially the well-dressed hearers, 'whene'er I mentioned hell to ears polite,' and urged that rude question, 'Do you deserve to be damned?'

We sang, rejoiced, and gave thanks at Mr. Stonehouse's; and again at Mrs. Hankinson's. I talked with one of her misses, to whom faith had come by hearing.

Wednesday, September 27. In our way to Oxford, I talked closely with my fellow traveller, Mr. Combes. He expressed his desire of faith: I was moved to sing 'Salvation by faith,' then 'Faith in Christ.' I told him, if the Spirit had convinced him of unbelief, He could of righteousness also, even before we reached Oxford. I stopped and prayed that he might believe. Immediately, he told me, he was in such a blessed temper as he never before experienced. We halted, and went to prayers. He testified the great delight he felt, saying, it was heaven, if it would but continue. While we were discoursing, the fire within him, he said, diffused itself through every part; he was brim-full of joy (yet not knowing he believed), and eager to praise God. He called upon me to join. 'Was I now in heaven, I could not think of my sins; I should only think of praising God.' We sang and shouted all the way to Oxford.

I met our friends with Mr. Hutchins's at Fox's. Mrs. Platt was full of life and love. We read the experiences of the Moravians.

Thursday, September 28. I called on my friend that *was,* John Sarney, now entirely estranged by the offence of the cross. I rode to my *constant* friend, John Gambold. Mr. Combes communicated with us: his warmth, he told me, had returned through his *professing* his faith. I left Mrs. Gambold in confident hope of soon receiving it. I preached boldly at Oxford; prayed after God with Mr. Wells.

Saturday, September 30. I returned to town, having in some measure confirmed our friends at Oxford. My brother informed me of one who was yesterday an open sinner, and to-day received into Christ's church, or the company of faithful people. Mrs. Claggett said that this morning, in utter despair, she had heard a distinct whisper, 'I am the Lord thy God, mighty to save.'

Sunday, October 1. I read prayers and gave the sacrament at the questroom. In the afternoon I read prayers, and preached at St. Margaret's, Westminster.

Monday, October 2. I dined at Mr. Brockmar's; and we admonished one another in psalms and hymns and spiritual songs. I went, with the three Miss Claggetts, to our poor sick woman. My brother and James followed; then Mrs. Metcalf and three of the Delamottes. We found her full of triumph, and vehement desires to be dissolved, and to be with Christ. We did this in remembrance of Him.

Thursday, October 5. I went with Sparks to Newgate; shamefully unwilling: yet preached on repentance with earnest zeal.

Sunday, October 8. I preached at Bexley 'all under sin'; finished my sermon in the afternoon. The people very outrageous. Mrs. Delamotte carried me home. I exhorted my friends in the kitchen. A sermon was read in the parlour. I preached faith in Christ. Mr. Delamotte made no objection, but seemed much pleased.

Monday, October 9. I walked with Will Delamotte to Bexley, where my sermon has occasioned a great uproar.

Wednesday, October 11. I got back to my friends in London. I spoke plainly to Mr. Claggett, who has been very violent toward his wife since I left them.

Thursday, October 12. I was at West's with Bray and Sparks, and prayed, pleading the promises in much bodily pain. I asked in faith that it might leave me: it did, while I was walking to James's.

Friday, October 13. At seven I read prayers and preached at St. Antholin's.

Sunday, October 15. I heard Hutchins at St. Lawrence's: had much comfort and meltings in prayer after the sacrament. I preached the one thing needful at Islington, and added much extempore; sang at Mr. Stonehouse's: Sims's was excessively crowded in the evening; spake with much boldness and warmth. At Bray's I found the bands meeting. Mr. Stonehouse was there, in a most childlike spirit. I was moved to pray for him earnestly, and according to God. I asked particularly that some one might *then* receive the atonement. While they were going, E___ came; complained of the pain and burden of sin that bruised him. I took him aside with Hutchins. He received faith in immediate answer to our prayer; professed it; full of peace, and joy, and love. I expressed a strong desire to pray for Mr. Stonehouse. I prayed again with vehemence and tears. Bray was greatly affected; so were James and all the rest: yet no answer. Mr. Stonehouse said the blessing was withheld from him to increase our importunity.

Friday, October 20. Seeing so few present at St. Antholin's, I thought of preaching extempore: afraid; yet ventured on the promise, 'Lo, I am with you always;' and spake on justification from Rom. iii., for three-quarters of an hour, without hesitation. Glory be to God, who keepeth His promise for ever.

Saturday, October 21. I waited with my brother on the Bishop of London, to answer the complaints he had heard against us, that we preached an absolute assurance of salvation. Some of his words were, 'If by "assurance" you mean an inward persuasion, whereby a man is conscious in himself, after examining his life by the law of God, and weighing his own sincerity, that he is in a state of salvation, and acceptable to God, I don't see how any good Christian can be without such an assurance.' 'This,' we answered, 'is what we contend for: but we have been charged as Antinomians, for preaching justification by faith only.' 'Can any one preach otherwise, who agrees to our Church and the Scriptures?' 'Indeed, by preaching it strongly, and not inculcating good works, many have been made Antinomians in theory, though not in practice: especially in King Charles's time.' 'But there is a heavy charge against us Bishops, by your bringing the Archbishop's authority for rebaptizing an adult.' My brother answered that he had expressly declared the contrary: 'yet,' added he, 'if a person dissatisfied with lay-baptism should desire episcopal, I should think it my duty to administer it, after having acquainted the Bishop according to the canon.' 'Well; I am against it myself, where any one has had the Dissenters baptism.'

Next my brother inquired whether his reading in a Religious Society made it a conventicle. His Lordship warily referred us to the laws: but upon our urging the question, 'Are the Religious Societies conventicles?' he answered, 'No; I think not: however, you can read the acts and laws as well as I: I determine nothing.' We hoped his Lordship would not henceforward receive an accusation against a presbyter, but at the mouth of two or three witnesses.

He said, 'No; by no means. And you may have free access to me at all times.' We thanked him, and took our leave.

Sunday, October 22. I preached one thing needful at St. Clement's, to a very large audience (many of whom stayed the communion), and again at Sir G. Wheler's chapel.

Tuesday, October 24. I told Mr. Claggett, in one of his persecuting fits, that I should be glad to see him when on a sick-bed; that I had the satisfaction of having him my friend when he was most so to himself and to God. He went out to fetch Bishop Taylor to confute me; but opened upon a place strongly asserting this living, justifying faith. He owned himself fully convinced; admired the hand of Providence; confessed he had loathed the sight of me, and hated me from his heart; but now loved me entirely, and all mankind; could hug me in his bosom; never knew such comfort in his life as at this moment; could not be beat out of it by all the world. Alas! that this morning-cloud should ever pass away!

Thursday, October 26. At Mrs. Hind's I was charged by Mr. Capell with particularly pleading the promises. I confessed, and justified it. James came to second me. We were both zealous, not angry.

Friday, October 27. I was at Mr. Sparks's, who is fully persuaded his sins are forgiven.

Sunday, October 29. I preached with strength at St. George's; then at Ironmongers Almshouses; and at night expounded Rom. v. to a large audience in the Minories.

Thursday, November 2. I was much affected in praying for Mr. Stonehouse.

Friday, November 3. I sang with him; envied his exquisite tenderness of conscience. I walked with Metcalf and Betty Claggett to visit a woman dying in the faith; thence to Miss Reeves, who is now assured of her acceptance with God.

Saturday, November 4. I preached at St. Antholin's, reconciling those who never differed, St. Paul and St. James.

Sunday, November 5. I preached the three fold state at St. Alban's, Wood Street: then expounded at Sims's.

Tuesday, November 7. At Newgate I was melted down under the word I spake.

Wednesday, November 8. At Bexley. Mr. Piers, through fear of the world's threatenings, had left off the meeting on Wednesday night. My sister would not give up her pretensions to faith; told me, half angry, Well, you will know in the next world whether I have faith or no. I asked her, Will you then discharge me, in the sight of God, from speaking to you again? If you will, I promise never more to open my mouth till we meet in eternity. She burst into tears, fell on my neck, and melted me into fervent prayer for her.

Saturday, November 11. Charles Graves came, and rejoiced my heart with the account of his having received the atonement.

Sunday, November 12. Mr. Piers refused me his pulpit, through fear of man, pretending tenderness to his flock. I plainly told him, if he so rejected my testimony, I would come to see him no more. I walked back to town in the strength of the Lord, and expounded at Sims's. All were dissolved in tears.

Monday, November 13. Charles brought Mr. W. Seward; a zealous soul, knowing only the baptism of John.

Tuesday, November 14. I had another conference with his Lordship of London. I have used your Lordship's permission to wait upon you. A woman desires me to baptize her; not being satisfied with her baptism by a Dissenter: she says sure and unsure is not the same. He immediately took fire, and interrupted me: 'I wholly disapprove of it: it is irregular.' 'My Lord, I did not expect your approbation. I only came, in obedience, to give you notice of my intention.' 'It is irregular. I never receive any such information, but from the minister.' 'My Lord, the Rubric does not so much as require the minister to give you notice, but any discreet person. I have the minister's leave.' 'Who gave you authority to baptize?' 'Your Lordship: and I shall exercise it in any part of the known world. Are you a licensed curate?' 'I have the leave of the proper minister.' 'But don't you know, no man can exercise parochial duty in London, without my leave? It is only *sub silentio*.' 'But you know many do take that permission for authority; and you yourself allow it.' 'It is one thing to connive, and another to approve. I have power to inhibit you.' 'Does your Lordship exert that power? Do you now inhibit me? Oh, why will you push things to an extreme? I do not inhibit you.' 'Why then, my Lord, according to your own concession, you permit or authorize me.' 'I have a power to punish, and to forbear punishing.' 'That seems to imply that I have done something worthy of punishment. I should be glad to know, that I may answer. Does your Lordship charge me with any crime?' 'No, no: I charge you with no crime.' 'Do you then dispense with my giving you notice of any baptisms for the future?' 'I neither dispense, nor not dispense.'

He railed at Lawrence on lay-baptism; blamed my brother's sermon, as inclining to Antinomianism. I charged Archbishop Tillotson with denying the faith. He allowed it, and owned they ran into one extreme to avoid another. He concluded the conference with, 'Well, sir, you knew my judgement before, and you know it now. Good morrow to you.'

I read prayers at Islington, and baptized an adult; Mr. Stonehouse, Mrs. Sims, and Mrs. Burton being the witnesses.

Wednesday, November 15. I dined at old Mr. Button's. They could scarcely be civil. Surely for Christ's sake have we lost this friendly family.

Thursday, November 16. After morning prayers, I baptized Mrs. Bell with hypothetical baptism. I sang and prayed with assistance, at Mr. Stonehouse's. Then Mrs. Wren confessed she had been in bondage ten years, but received the atonement on Tuesday night, while we were praying: was now perfectly free: full of peace, and joy in believing. Another professed her faith lately received. I dined at my friend Stonehouse's, who very kindly offers to keep my brother and me.

Mrs. Hankinson carried me to a poor woman, broken, bruised, and bound by sin. After prayer she arose, loosed from her bond, and glorified God.

Saturday, November 18. I had a joyful meeting with my dear Charles Delamotte, just returned from Georgia. I found, in conversation, that he had received forgiveness five months ago; and continued in peace and liberty.

Sunday, November 19. At Dr. Crow's desire, I preached in his church at Bishopsgate; and dined at Mr. Brockmar's, where Mr. Seward testified faith.

I visited a poor woman of eighty-four; who told me she was reserved for some work of God: was soon beat out of her own works; and in the midst of prayer set at liberty. She rose, caught hold of me, declared her enlargement; that she was now at ease, ready to go into eternity this moment. She prayed for and blessed me with great earnestness.

Monday, November 20. I had a most comfortable sacrament at Bray's; Mr. Sparks, the three Miss Claggetts, &c., partaking. I passed the evening at Blendon, in prayer and thanksgiving.

Tuesday, November 21. I communicated again at Bray's. I triumphed with some who are persecuted for righteousness sake.

Wednesday, November 22. I set out in the coach for Oxford.

Friday, November 24. I met Charles Kinchin there. I received the blessed sacrament at Mrs. Townsend's, with much comfort.

Saturday, November 25. I felt a pining desire to die, foreseeing the infinite dangers and troubles of life. At Mr. Wells's I preached *the* faith of the gospel to him and Mr. Hoare. Charles carried me to the Castle. I read prayers, and was afterwards constrained to speak freely and fully. I was much cheered by it myself. I rode with Mr. Wells and Kinchin to Coggs, where we spent the evening in prayer and the Scriptures.

Sunday, November 26. I preached the three fold state at Coggs: then rode on to my brother Gambold's.

Tuesday, November 28. I dined in ChristChurch Hall, as one not belonging to them.

Wednesday, November 29. After morning prayers, I called on Mr. Whitefield, who pressed me to accept of a College living. I read prayers, and preached at the Castle.

Thursday, November 30. I paid Mr. Gambold another visit, and parted with the sacrament.

Tuesday, December 5. I was at Convocation; where honest John Chicheley was presented with his degree; having before got orders, for which he came to England.

Thursday, December 7. I read prayers again to the poor prisoners in Bocardo.

Saturday, December 9. I was with the Dean; who complained of my brother's obscurity in his sermon on salvation; and expressly denied the assurance of faith, and earnest of the Spirit.

Sunday, December 10. I preached at the Castle, 'All under sin,' and helped to administer the sacrament. I read prayers, and preached there again in the afternoon.

Monday, December 11. I came in the coach to Wycombe. I lodged at Mr. Hollis's, who entertained me with his French Prophets equal, in his account, if not superior, to the Old Testament ones. While we were undressing, he fell into violent agitations, and gobbled like a turkey-cock. I was frightened, and began exorcising him with 'Thou deaf and dumb devil,' &c. He soon recovered out of his fit of inspiration. I prayed, and went to bed, not half liking my bedfellow. I did not sleep very sound with Satan so near me. I got to London by one the next day. George Whitefield came to J. Bray's soon after me. I was full of vehement desire in prayer. I heard him preach to a vast throng at St. Helen's.

Thursday, December 14. I heard a glorious account of the success of the gospel at Islington. Some of the fiercest opposers are converted.

Friday, December 15. At Mr. Stonehouse's I met Mrs. Vaughan, full of joy in the Holy Ghost, but not without a mixture of nature.

Saturday, December 16. Hester Hobson and her sister called, being sick of love to Christ crucified. My soul, in and after prayer with them, was all desire and expectation.

Sunday, December 17. I met Mr. Broughton at Mrs. Hind's. The last time we had parted good friends, and he thanked me for my friendly offices with Miss Reeves. He now desired me to get from her a discharge.

Monday, December 18. She told me she fully released him from his promises, but durst not give him a written discharge, lest her brother should cast her off.

Tuesday, December 19. I asked my friend Stonehouse, 'Dost thou believe in the Son of God?' And he could confidently answer, 'Yes, I do, and now know that I believe.' We sang (Mrs. Hankinson joining us) in the spirit of faith, and triumphed in the name of the Lord our God.

Thursday, December 21. At St. Antholin's the clerk asked me my name, and said, 'Dr. Venn has forbidden any Methodist to preach. Do you call yourself a Methodist?' 'I do not: the world may call me what they please.' 'Well, sir,' said he, 'it is pity the people should go away without preaching. You may preach.' I did so, on good works.

Saturday, December 23. I was deeply affected in singing at Blendon: retired, and poured out my soul in prayer for love.

Christmas Day. I preached at Islington in the morning, and gave the cup; George Stonehouse in the afternoon.

Tuesday, December 26. George Whitefield preached. We had the sacrament this and the four following days. On Thursday my brother preached; on Friday, George Whitefield; and on Saturday, Mr. Robson. The whole week was a festival indeed; a joyful season, holy unto the Lord.

Tuesday, January 2. I was at Mr. Stone house's, with Mrs. Vaughan and others. I urged him to throw away his mystics; but he adhered to them with the greater obstinacy. I saw myself in him.

Wednesday, January 3. To-day our sister Butcher died (the first that has) triumphant in the faith. At five she said, 'I trust only to the blood of Christ. I cast myself at His feet; and if I perish, I perish.' Soon after, 'Now I am sure of heaven.' Her last breath was spent in exhorting her husband and the rest to confide in Jesus Christ.

Friday, January 5. My brother, Mr. Seward, Hall, Whitefield, Ingham, Kinchin, Hutchins, all set upon me; but I could not agree to settle at Oxford without farther direction from God.

Saturday, January 6. Mr. Sparks and I were at Mr. Howard's; who denied any real communion we can have with God.

Sunday, January 7. I was offended much at some orders which Bray, &c., were imposing on the Society.

Wednesday, January 10. I met Mr. Broughton, who laboured hard to persuade me to make affidavit of what Miss Reeves had said. I positively refused it, as treachery to her, both in him and me.

Mr. Thorold expounded at the Society. We had some discourse about agitations: no sign of grace, in my humble opinion.

Thursday, January 11. I met a Moravian and his wife. She related her genuine conversion: had received forgiveness *before* the abiding witness of the Spirit.

Saturday, January 13. Pierced with the prayers of Hester Hobson, I expected a fresh manifestation of Christ continually: which I found the next day at the sacrament.

Monday, January 15. I was at Mr. Stonehouse's when Mr. Silvester came. Mr. Stonehouse insisted upon choosing a Lecturer himself. I attended him to Mr. Lloyd, the Reader. We had close talk of faith. Both he and Mrs. Lloyd are convinced.

Tuesday, January 16. I prayed in faith for her. Immediately she was filled with comfort. I called on Mr. Wilde, who tells me he lately received forgiveness under my sermon.

Wednesday, January 17. George Whitefield gave us so promising account of Oxford, that I found myself strongly inclined to go.

Sunday, January 21. I was much affected under Mr. Stonehouse's sermon. I preached myself in the afternoon, to a crowded church, on justification by faith.

Monday, January 22. Lady Crisp sent for me. I went, and found Mr. Stonehouse there. She behaved with great courtesy. I transcribed an hymn for Miss. After supper, her Ladyship spoke largely in praise of marriage. I saw, and pitied, my poor friend, sorely beset. We sang. It was late before we parted.

Tuesday, January 23. Mrs. Vaughan seemed deeply humbled, under a sense of her late vain, confident delusions.

Wednesday, January 24. I expounded (for the benefit of two clergymen present), 'Know ye not, that your bodies are the temples of the Holy Ghost?' and proved the promise of the Spirit to all, both from Scripture and our own Church.

Thursday, January 25. I expounded at Brockmar's. The Lord was present. A woman stopped me departing; confessed herself under the full power of the devil; fell at my feet. We prayed in confidence. On my mentioning in prayer the absolved adulteress, she cried out, 'I have received the comfort!' I rose full of love, and joy, and triumph: whereof we were all partakers.

I was sent for to Bray: the three Miss Newtons were there. I expounded again with power.

Friday, January 26. At Dr. Newton's I sang and prayed with them: much affected now; well pleased last night.

Saturday, January 27. I carried Bray to Mrs. Whitcomb's; the Claggetts, Metcalf, and his mother, and Hester Hobson were there. We communicated, prayed, and sang with great life and comfort. I slept at Blendon.

Sunday, January 28. I preached on 'the three states' at Bexley. Some went out of church: and more in the afternoon, while I expounded, 'Woe is unto me, if I preach not the gospel.' I was quite spent; yet renewed my strength for the poor people at night.

Wednesday, January 31. I told Mr. Delamotte he was not converted, had not the Spirit, or faith, and begged him to pray God to show him wherein he was wanting. He could not receive my saying, yet was not angry. Mrs. Delamotte was quite transported with joy and love. In the stage-coach with my sister Kez, I found three women, and was very loath to speak; yet broke through, and laboured to convince them of sin and of righteousness. They all assented to the truth, and were, I hope, in some measure awakened to pursue the one thing needful. I left Kez at my aunt's, in Islington. I assisted to expound at the Society, and slept at J. Bray's in peace.

Friday, February 2. With Charles Metcalf I visited that worthy man, Zouberbuhler, in the Marshalsea for debt; much moved at his afflictions.

Sunday, February 4. At night walked over the fields from Islington, several of us, with the voice of joy and thanksgiving.

Thursday, February 8. I carried Zouberbuhler the news of his goods being redeemed by Mr. Seward. I visited him again on Saturday, and was drawn in compassion towards him, and faith for him. At Islington I rejoiced over a dying believer.

Saturday, February 10. I expounded to many hundreds at a Society in Beech Lane.

Sunday, February 11. We prayed for utterance this day. My brother preached. I was comforted in the sacrament. I prayed again at Mr. Stonehouse's for a blessing upon my ministry. (Lady Crisp with my brother.)

I read prayers, and preached without notes on blind Bartimeus, the Lord being greatly my helper. Let Him have all the glory. I returned to pray at Mr. Stonehouse's. Miss Crisp asked to be admitted. We had close searching talk, before I expounded to the Society.

Monday, February 12. Mrs. Wheeler tells me, she received Christ last Saturday, being weighed down with the fear of death, and de livered in a moment; melted into love; able to apply Christ and all the promises to herself. Mr. Stonehouse informed me of a woman who had rejected him last week; but now sent for him, received the sacrament, was reconciled to God and him, and died in peace.

Tuesday, February 13. I read a letter from Sarah Hurst, pressing me to Oxford, and Cowley (which is now vacant). Quite resigned, I offered myself; opened the book upon those words, 'With stammering lips, and with another tongue will He speak to this people.' I thought it a prohibition, yet continued without a will. I was with Captain Flatman at the Marshalsea; read prayers, and preached from Luke vii. 36, the woman washing Christ's feet. The word was with power, all were attentive and thankful. I visited Zouberbuhler, removed to the Fleet.

Wednesday, February 14. I read prayers at Newgate, and preached the law first, and then the gospel. We sang, 'Invitation to sinners.' All were affected.

Thursday, February 15. I preached again at the Marshalsea. I was sent for by an harlot (supposed to be dying), and preached Christ, the friend of sinners, I trust to her heart. I read prayers at Islington. Miss Crisp asked me home. My Lady was there. We had pertinent discourse. The younger went with me to Mrs. Hankinson's; extremely desirous of faith. I prayed for her with great earnestness. At the Society I expounded the woman of Samaria. When I had done, she ran to me, and cried, 'I do, I do believe! Those words which you spoke came with power, "Him that cometh unto Me, I will in no wise cast out." An unknown peace flowed with them into my soul.' We sang, rejoiced, and gave thanks to the pardoning God in her behalf.

Sunday, February 18. I preached at Islington, on the woman that *was* a sinner; at the Marshalsea, from Rom. iii. I prayed by the sick woman: expounded at Sims's to two several companies.

Monday, February 19. I prayed in the prison with Anne Dodd, well-disposed, weary of sin, longing to break loose. I preached powerfully on the last day. I prayed after God for the poor harlots. Our sisters carried away one in triumph. I followed to Mrs. Hanson's, who took charge of the returning prodigal. Our hearts were overflowed with pity for her. She seemed confounded, silent, testifying her joy and love by her tears only. We sang and prayed over her in great confidence.

At three I met Miss Crisp at Mrs. Claggett's, who helped me to rejoice for the lost sheep which I have found. In the evening I expounded at Mr. Hind's. A lady was deeply wounded.

Tuesday, February 20. I waked full of concern for the poor harlot; and began an hymn for her. At five I called on Miss Crisp; then on Mr. Stonehouse, where I expounded the woman taken in adultery.

Wednesday, February 21. I heard that Cowley living was disposed of; and rejoiced. With my brother I waited on the Archbishop. He showed us great affection; spoke mildly of Mr. Whitefield; cautioned us to give no more umbrage than was necessary for our own defence; to forbear exceptionable phrases; to keep to the doctrines of the Church. We told him we expected persecution; would abide by the Church till her Articles and Homilies were repealed. He assured us he knew of no design in the governors of the Church to innovate; and neither should there be any innovation while he lived: avowed justification by faith only; and his joy to see us as often as we pleased.

From him we went to the Bishop of London; who denied his having condemned or even heard much of us. G. Whitefield's Journal, he said, was tainted with enthusiasm, though he was himself a pious, well-meaning youth. He warned us against Antinomianism, and dismissed us kindly.

I went in quest of a lost sheep, and found her coming with Bray from public prayers. She had been in deep distress; pierced with every word at the two last expoundings; almost fainted away this morning, weary and heavy-laden. She told Bray God could not forgive her, her sins were so great. She could not bear our triumph. We wrestled in prayer for her; and she declared her burden taken off, and her soul at peace. The more we prayed, the clearer still she was; till at last she testified that she did believe in Jesus with her whole heart. We continued in mighty prayer for all gross sinners; and I offered myself willingly to be employed peculiarly in their service.

Sunday, February 25. I preached justification by faith at Bexley. In the beginning of my discourse about twenty went out of church. They were better pleased with (or at least more patient of) me in the afternoon, while I preached on the woman at our Saviour's feet. Faint and spent at Blendon, I revived by exhorting above two hundred of the poor.

Monday, February 26. In our chapel I read Beveridge's sermon on the ministry, too much wanted by Betsy, and others, who are running into wild notions. The people came at night, and we were all comforted together by the word.

Wednesday, February 28. I met the bands at J. Bray's, and cautioned them against schism. I was violently opposed by one who should have seconded me. They urged me to go to Oxford: but I understood them, and begged to be excused.

Saturday, March 3. I expounded to upward of three hundred hearers at Beech Lane.

Sunday, March 4. I read prayers, and preached, and administered the sacrament at St. Catherine's; at Islington from John iii.; then expounded with much life at Mr. Sims's; and lastly at Mr. Bell's. I concluded the labour of the day with prayer among the bands.

Thursday, March 8. In the midst of earnest prayer at J. Bray's, a woman received power to become a child of God.

Saturday, March 10. I went to Newgate with my usual reluctance; preached with freedom; and in prayer had great power, as all present seemed to confess. I expounded at Beech Lane: in prayer I asked some token, if our gospel really is a ministration of the Spirit; and I inquired if any had received an answer. One, and another, and another testified their sense of the divine presence. We rejoiced as men that divide the spoil.

Sunday, March 11. I preached justification at St. Catherine's. I baptized two women at Islington (five adults I baptized some time before), and preached with great liberty from the woman of Samaria. My friend Stonehouse was very peevish with me for a trifle, and very warm. I kept my temper, but was hindered in my expounding by his disputes. I encouraged Miss Crisp, now persecuted by her relations. I envied the dead at Mrs. Vaughan's. I had serious talk with Stonehouse, in defence of Miss Crisp. Both were humbled.

Monday, March 12. I was at Newgate with Bray. I prayed, sang, exhorted with great life and vehemence. I talked in the cells to two Papists, who renounced all merit but that of Jesus Christ. I expounded at Bray's on the day of judgement. The power of the Lord was present to wound. A woman cried out as in an agony. Another sank down overpowered. All were moved and melted, as wax before the fire. At eight I expounded on Dowgate Hill. Two were then taken into the fold.

Wednesday, March 14. I found one of the Papists full of peace and joy in believing, immediately after we prayed.

Tuesday, March 20. A double power and blessing accompanied my word at Fetter Lane.

Thursday, March 22. I was at the Marshalsea with Mr. Oakley. I prayed with the sick; read prayers, and expounded the lesson.

Sunday, March 25. Betty Hopson came, and prayed that to-day we might have a feast of fat things. Mr. Stonehouse was full of love, and preached an excellent sermon on faith. After the sacrament we continued our triumph. I preached with power, 'Lazarus raised.' Then sang and prayed at the room. Great was our rejoicing in the Lord. I buried a corpse, and exhorted the congregation. I expounded at Mr. Stonehouse's with great enlargement. An opposer was troublesome, till we prayed him down. I visited Mr. Lloyd, and then Mrs. Vaughan, both as full of love and joy as they could contain. By midnight I rested with Oakley at J. Bray's.

Tuesday, March 27. At Mr. Crouch's I expounded on persecution. A man cried out, 'That's a lie.' We betook ourselves to prayer and singing. The shout of a King was in the midst of us. The man came up quite aSable. Another asked what that comfort and joy meant: I calmly invited him to experience it.

Wednesday, March 28. We dissuaded my brother from going to Bristol, from an unaccount able fear that it would prove fatal to him. A great power was among us. He offered himself willingly to whatsoever the Lord should

114

appoint. The next day he set out, commended by us to the grace of God. He left a blessing behind. I desired to die with him.

Sunday, April 1. I preached at St. Catherine's, where I met my old friend Mrs. Paine, of East Grinstead. I administered the sacrament. I dined at Chrissy Anderson's; went in a coach with her and Esther to Islington; comforted in the way while singing. I expounded the good Samaritan, with divine assistance. I prayed at Fetter Lane that the Lord might be in the midst of us; received a remarkable answer. B. Nowers, in strong pangs, groaned, screamed, roared out. I was not offended by it nor edified. We sang and praised God with all our might. I could not get home till eleven.

Wednesday, April 4. At Mr. West's I rejoiced over an happy soul, who received faith under my last expounding.

Friday, April 6. I convinced a woman of sin; found another convinced of righteousness. A man who had rejected me was now overpowered. Mrs. Daniel and Winstone were apprehended by Christ.

Sunday, April 15. At Islington in the vestry, the churchwardens demanded my licence. I wrote down my name; preached with increase of power, on the woman taken in adultery. None went out. I gave the cup. At night I waited upon Count Zinzendorf with Bray and Hutton. He received us very cordially; told us of six hundred Moors converted, two hundred Greenlanders, three hundred Hottentots. *Saluta meo nomine fratres et sorores. Christi Spiritum illis apprecor.*

We found his prayers answered at the Society. Two received forgiveness; many were filled with unutterable groanings; all received some spiritual gift. We could not part; but continued our triumph till the morning.

Monday, April 16. The Count visited us in Fetter Lane, and answered the several questions we proposed to him. To-day I first saw Miss Raymond and Mr. Rogers, at the expounding.

Tuesday, April 17. I tried in vain to check Mr. Shaw in his wild rambling talk against the Christian priesthood. At last I told him I would oppose him to the utmost; and either he or I must quit the Society.

I assisted Mr. Stonehouse again (as every day this great and holy week) in administering the sacrament. The presence of the Lord was much with us; and again at night, in the word expounded.

Wednesday, April 18. I met Shaw at James's. He insisted that there is no priesthood; but he himself could baptize and administer the other sacrament as well as any man. At Mrs. Claggett's I met Mr. Rogers and Miss Raymond; and prayed earnestly for her.

In my expounding, I warned them strongly against schism; into which Shaw's notions must necessarily lead. The Society were all for my brother's immediate return.

Thursday, April 19. I found Mr. Stonehouse exactly right: warned Mrs. Vaughan (Hunter, half -perverted) and Brockmars against Shaw's pestilent errors, and spoke strongly at the Savoy Society, in behalf of the Church of England.

Good Friday, April 20. Mrs. Acourt was this day justified, in answer to our prayer. I felt life under Mr. Stonehouse's sermon. From church I went to the house to pray. J. Bray gave me the Gospel for the day to expound. I besought them, in strong words, not to rend the seamless coat by their divisions. J. Bray himself, that pillar of our Church, begins to shake. At night I preached to the Society in Wapping.

Saturday, April 21. I was with James at the Count's, who spoke much against the intended separation of our brethren. I met Metcalf, wholly perverted, a rank Quaker!

Easter Day, April 22. I talked with the Count, about motions, visions, dreams, and was confirmed in my dislike to them.

Wednesday, April 25. I began Potter on Church Government: a seasonable antidote against the growing spirit of delusion. I heard G. Whitefield, very powerful, at Fetter Lane. I was with him and Howel Harris, a man after my own heart. George related the dismal effects of Shaw's doctrine at Oxford. Both Howel and he insisted on Shaw's expulsion from the Society. Poor Metcalf had little to say for his friend and master.

Friday, April 27. I heard G. Whitefield in Islington churchyard. The numerous congregation could not have been more affected within the walls. I exhorted them at Fetter Lane to continue steadfast in the means of grace.

Saturday, April 28. Mr. Stonehouse was much concerned that we should so misunderstand, as if he had forbid G. Whitefield's preaching in his church. To-day he preached out again. After him, Bowers got up to speak: I conjured him not; but he beat me down, and *followed his impulse.* I carried many away with me. In the evening I expounded at Exall's. A woman received the atonement.

Sunday, April 29. At Islington vestry the churchwardens forbad my preaching: demanded my local licence. I said nothing but that 'I heard them.' Scions was very abusive; bidding me shake off the dust of my feet, &c.; and said, 'You have all the spirit of the devil,' mentioning Mr. Whitefield, Stonehouse, and me by name.

After prayers Mr. Stonehouse made way for me to the pulpit: I offered to go up, when one Cotteril, and a beadle, forcibly kept me back. I thought of, 'The servant of the Lord must not strive,' and yielded. Mr. Streat preached. I assisted at the sacrament. I preached afterwards at our house, and prayed fervently for the opposers. I waited on Justice Elliot. He had gone with Sir John Gunson into the vestry, and severely chid the churchwardens; who had made the clerk read the canon, call a vestry, &c. Mr. Streat advised to ask Mr. Stonehouse to discharge me from ever preaching again.

In the afternoon Scions abused Streat himself at the vestry; abused us; owned he said, 'the devil was in us all.' I read prayers; Mr. Scott preached. At night I was greatly strengthened to expound, and pray for our persecutors.

All were mild and peaceable among the bands. I heard that George had had above ten thousand hearers.

Monday, April 30. I preached at the Marshalsea. Mr. Stonehouse told us he had been with the Bishop, but left him close, shut up, sour, refusing to answer but to the written case. At James's I rejoiced to find Charles Metcalf coming back.

Tuesday, May 1. During the time of prayers the churchwardens still kept guard on the pulpit-stairs. I was not inclined to fight my way through them. Mr. Stonehouse preached a thundering sermon (unless their consciences are seared). I took notes of it. I took water with James for Hastings. A poor harlot was struck down by the word. She, and all, were melted into tears, and prayers, and strong cries for her. I have a good hope this brand will also be plucked out of the fire.

Wednesday, May 2. She was at Fetter Lane, where I expounded the prodigal.

Thursday, May 10. I expounded at Blendon; many fine folk from Eltham attending.

Friday, May 11. I prayed at Welling, with a dying man, full of humility, and faith, and love.

Sunday, May 13. I was enabled to discourse from the prodigal, at Bexley.

Monday, May 14. At West's my mouth was opened to expound Rom. viii. Miss Raymond was among my hearers.

Tuesday, May 15. She was brought so strongly to my mind, that I was even constrained to pray for her with tears.

Wednesday, May 16. I preached with power and freedom in the Marshalsea. I prayed by Mrs. Cameron, who owned herself convinced. She had been a Deist, because it is so incredible the Almighty God should condescend to die for His creatures.

I attended G. Whitefield to Blackheath. He preached in the rain to many listening sinners. At Fetter Lane a dispute arose about lay-preaching. Many, particularly Bray and Fish, were very zealous for it. Mr. Whitefield and I declared against it.

Saturday, May 19. At the Common, George preached from 'The Holy Ghost shall come upon thee.' In the evening I found my brother at Mr. Hodges's.

Sunday, May 20. I received the sacrament at St. Paul's, with best part of our Society.

Monday, May 21. At Mrs. Claggett's I found Miss Raymond, Rogers, J. Cennick, Harris, Whitefield, Piriam, Mason, the Delamottes. Mr. Claggett was very friendly, and invited me to Broadoaks.

Tuesday, May 22. Miss Raymond carried me in her coach to Islington. My friend Stonehouse was delighted to see me. We sang together and prayed, as in the months that are past.

Thursday, May 24. J. Bray took upon him to reprove me for checking the course of the Spirit. I made him no answer; but I believe not every spirit; nor any till I have tried it by the fruits and the written Word.

I met Miss Raymond (as almost every day), and joined with her and our friends in prayer and singing. Mr. Claggett pressed me now, with the utmost importunity, to go with him to morrow.

Friday, May 25. At noon I set out on horse back; our sisters in the chaise. By two the next day we surprised Miss Betty at Broadoaks. I was full of prayer that the Lord would gather a church in this place.

Sunday, May 27. Still Mr. Claggett opposed my preaching. I went to church, where I preached the new birth. We returned singing. Mr. Claggett still more violent. I told him, he was doing the devil's work. Between jest and earnest, he struck me; raged exceedingly to see the people come flocking to the word. God gave me utterance to make known the mystery of the gospel to four or five hundred listening souls.

Tuesday, May 29. Franklyn, a farmer, in vited me to preach in his field. I did so, to about five hundred, on, Repent, for the kingdom of heaven is at hand. I returned to the house rejoicing.

Wednesday, May 30. I convinced a sick man of unbelief. Another on his death-bed received forgiveness, and witnessed a good confession. I invited near a thousand sinners (with whom the whole house was filled at night) to come weary and heavy-laden to Christ for rest.

Thursday, May 31. A Quaker sent me a pressing invitation to preach at Thackstead. I scrupled preaching in another's parish, till I had been refused the church. Many Quakers, and near seven hundred others, attended, while I declared in the highways, 'The Scripture hath concluded all under sin.'

Friday, June 1. My subject, to above one thousand attentive sinners, was, 'He shall save His people from their sins.' Many showed their emotion by their tears.

Saturday, June 2. At six I set out for London, with a quiet mind, leaving my beloved friends in the hands of God. The first thing I heard in town was that my poor friend Stonehouse was actually married. It is a satisfaction to me that I had no hand in it.

Sunday, June 3. G. Whitefield advised me (I thank him for his love) to follow Mr. Stonehouse's example. He preached in the morning in Moorfields, and in the evening at Kennington Common, to an innumerable multitude.

Monday, June 4. I walked with a young Quaker to Islington church. Satan hindered me; so Mr. Scott baptized him. He told me afterwards, 'When the words were speaking, I sensibly found the Holy Ghost descend into my soul; the joy rose higher and higher, till at last I could neither speak nor move; but seemed rapt into the third heaven.'

I had some conversation with Mrs. Stonehouse; surely a gracious, lovely soul; then with him. We joined in prayer; and I was better reconciled to their sudden marriage. I met Shaw, the self-ordained priest. He was brim-full of proud wrath and fierceness. His spirit suited to his principles. I could do him no good; but was kept calm and benevolent towards him; therefore he could do me no harm. I stood by G. Whitefield while he preached on the mount in

Blackheath. The cries of the wounded were heard on every side. What has Satan gained by turning him out of the churches?

Tuesday, June 5. I was with him at Blendon. Bowers and Bray followed us thither, drunk with the spirit of delusion. George honestly said, 'They were two grand enthusiasts.'

Wednesday, June 6. Above sixty of the poor people had passed the night in Mr. Delamotte's barn, singing and rejoicing. I sang and prayed with them before the door. George's exhortation left them all in tears.

At the Society in the evening, Shaw pleaded for his spirit of prophecy; charged me with love of pre-eminence; with making my prose lytes twofold more children of the devil than before. Fish said he looked upon me as de livered over to Satan, &c. They declared them selves no longer members of the Church of England. We were kept tolerably meek; and parted at eleven. Now am I clear of them. By renouncing the Church, they have discharged me.

Thursday, June 7. Many of our friends have been pestered by the French Prophets, and such-like *pretenders* to inspiration. J. Bray is the foremost to listen to them, and often carried away with their delusions. To-day I had the happiness to find at his house the famous Prophetess Lavington. She was sitting by Bowers; and Mrs. Sellers on the other side. The Prophet Wise asked, 'Can a man attain perfection here?' I answered, 'No.' The Prophetess began groaning. I turned, and said, 'If you have anything to speak, speak it.' She lifted up her voice, like the lady on the tripod, and cried out vehemently, 'Look for perfection; I say absolute perfection!' I was minded to rebuke her; but God gave me uncommon recollection, and command of spirit, so that I sat quiet, and replied not. I offered at last to sing, which she allowed, but did not join. Bray pressed me to stay, and hear her pray. They knelt; I stood. She prayed most pompously, addressing to Bray with particular encomiums. I durst not say Amen. She concluded with an horrible hellish laugh; and endeavoured to turn it off. She showed violent displeasure against our baptized Quaker, saying, 'God had showed her, He would destroy all outward things.'

Friday and *Saturday, June* 8 and 9. I took the deposition of Anne Graham, Mrs. Biddle, and Mrs. Rigby, concerning her lewd life and conversation; and warned our friends everywhere against her. I joined at West's with Hutchins and Miss Kinchin, in earnest prayer for the promise of the Father.

Whit Sunday, June 10. I read the Society my account of the Prophetess. All were shocked but poor J. Bray. He now *appeared,* and strongly withstood me, and vindicated that Jezebel. I gave no place to him, no, not for a moment. My natural temper was kept down, and changed into a passionate concern for him, which I expressed in prayers and tears. All besides him were melted down. I kissed him, and testified my love; but could make no impression.

Monday, June 11. I expounded with great liberty of spirit; and found the blessing of opposition.

Tuesday, June 12. I heard more of my prophetess, who told a brother that she can command Christ to come to her in what shape she pleases; as a dove, an eagle, &c. The devil owed her a shame by bringing her again to Bray's. Wise, her gallant, came first; whom I urged with a plain question, whether he had or had not cohabited with her. He was *forced* to confess he had. J. Bray was vehement in her defence; when she came in, flew upon us like a tigress; tried to outface me; insisted that she was immediately inspired. I prayed. She cried, 'The devil was in me. I was a fool, a blockhead, a blind leader of the blind; put out the people's eyes,' &c. She roared outrageously; said it was the lion in her. (True; but not the Lion of Judah.) She *would* come to the Society in spite of me: if not, they would all go down.

I asked, 'Who is on God's side? Who for the old Prophets rather than the new? Let them follow me.' They followed me into the preaching-room. I prayed, and expounded the lesson with extraordinary power. The women, several of them, gave an account of their conversion through my ministry. Our dear brother Bowers confessed himself convinced of his error. We rejoiced and triumphed in the name of the Lord our God.

Wednesday, June 13. My brother returned. We had over the Prophetess's affair before the Society. Bray and Bowers were much humbled. All agreed to disown the Prophetess. Brother Hall proposed expelling Shaw and Wolf. We consented, *nem. con.*, that their names should be erased out of the Society-book, because they disowned themselves members of the Church of England.

Thursday, June 14. I heard my brother preach on Blackheath, 'Christ our wisdom, righteousness, sanctification, and redemption.' We continued at the Green Man's, singing and rejoicing. George Whitefield gave a lively exhortation to about thirty of us. I slept with Seward and my brother.

Friday, June 15. The last time I had met Mr. Stonehouse and our opposers in the vestry, he astonished by telling me, 'He had consented that I should preach no more.' I thought in myself, 'What is man? or what is friendship?' and said nothing. To-day, in company with my brother and him, I mentioned, without in tending it, my exclusion through his consent. He pleaded that the Bishop of London had justified his churchwardens in their forcible expulsion of me; but at last was quite melted down; would do anything to repair his fault; resolved no other should be excluded by him, as I had been.

Sunday, June 17. My brother preached to above ten thousand people (as was supposed) in Moorfields, and to a still larger congregation on Kennington Common. I preached twice in the prison.

Monday, June 18. I sang and prayed at Mrs. Euster's a lively, gracious soul; but too apt to depend on her inward feelings.

Tuesday, June 19. I was at Lambeth with Mr. Piers. His Grace expressly forbad him to let any of us preach in his church: charged us with breach of the canon. I mentioned the Bishop of London's authorizing my forcible exclusion. He would not hear me; said he did not dispute. He asked me what call I had. I answered, 'A dispensation of the gospel is committed to me.' 'That is, to St. Paul; but I do not dispute: and will not proceed to excommunication YET.' 'Your Grace has taught me in your book on Church Government, that a man unjustly excommunicated is not thereby cut off from communion with Christ.' 'Of that I am the judge.' I asked him. if Mr. Whitefield's success was not a spiritual sign, and sufficient proof of his call: recommended Gamaliel's advice. He dismissed us; Piers, with kind professions; me, with all the marks of his displeasure.

I felt nothing in my heart but peace. I prayed and sang at Bray's: but some hours after, at West's, sank down in great heaviness and discouragement. I found a little relief from the scripture that first offered: Acts xvii. 3, 'Opening and alleging, that Christ must needs have suffered, and risen again from the dead; and that this Jesus, whom I preach unto von, is Christ.'

Friday, June 22. The sower of tares is beginning to trouble us with disputes about predestination. My brother was wonderfully owned at Wapping last week, while asserting the contrary truth. To-night I asked in prayer that if God would have all men to be saved, He would show some token for good upon us. Three were justified in immediate answer to that prayer. We prayed again; several fell down under the power of God, present to witness His universal love.

Saturday, June 23. Some of the persons set at liberty came, and called on me to return Him thanks in their behalf. Twelve received forgiveness, it seems, last night; another in this hour. I dined at Mr. Stonehouse's. My inward conflict continued. I perceived it was the fear of man; and that, by preaching in the field next Sunday, as George Whitefield urges me, I shall break down the bridge, and become desperate. I retired, and prayed for particular direction; offering up my friends, my liberty, my life, for Christ's sake and the gospel's. I was somewhat less burdened; yet could not be quite easy, till I gave up all.

Sunday, June 24. St. John Baptist's day. The first scripture I cast my eye upon was 'Then came the servant unto Him, and said, Master, what shall we do?' I prayed with West, and went forth in the name of Jesus Christ. I found near ten thousand helpless sinners waiting for the Word, in Moorfields. I invited them in my Master's words, as well as name: Come unto Me, all ye that travail, and are heavy laden, and I will give you rest. The Lord was with me, even me, His meanest messenger, according to His promise. At St. Paul's, the Psalms, Lessons, &c., for the day put fresh life into me. So did the sacrament. My load was gone, and all my doubts and scruples. God shone upon my path; and I knew this was His will concerning me. At Newington, the rector, Mr. Motte, desired me to preach. My text was, 'All have sinned, and come short of the glory of God; being justified freely, &c.' I walked on to the Common, and cried to multitudes upon multitudes, 'Repent ye, and believe the gospel.' The Lord was my strength, and my mouth, and my wisdom. Oh that all would therefore praise the Lord for His goodness!

I was refreshed with the Society, at a primitive lovefeast.

Friday, June 29. At Wycombe I heard of much disturbance and sin, occasioned by Bowers's preaching in the streets. I reached Oxford the next day.

Saturday, June 30. I waited upon the Dean, who spoke with unusual severity against field-preaching and Mr. Whitefield: explained away all inward religion and union with God.

That the world, and their god, abhor our manner of acting, I have too sensible proof. This whole week has the messenger of Satan been buffeting me with uninterrupted temptation.

Sunday, July 1. I preached my sermon on justification before the University, with great boldness. All were very attentive. One could not help weeping. At night I received power to expound; several gownsmen were present; some mocked.

Monday, July 2. Mr. Gambold came. He had been with the Vice-Chancellor, and well received. I visited the Vice-Chancellor, at his own desire: gave him a full account of the Methodists; which he approved: but objected the irregularity of our doing good in other men's parishes; charged Mr. Whitefield with insincerity, and breach of promise; appealed to the Dean, and appointed a second meeting there. All were against my sermon, as liable to be misunderstood.

Tuesday, July 3. Poor wild Bowers had been laid hold on for preaching in Oxford. To-day the beadle brought him to me. I spoke to him very home. He had nothing to reply; but promised to do so no more, and thereby obtained his liberty.

At night I had another conference with the Dean, who cited Mr. Whitefield to judgement. I said, 'Mr. Dean, he shall be ready to answer your citation.' He used his utmost address to bring me off from preaching abroad, from expounding in houses, from singing psalms: denied justification by faith only, and all vital religion: promised me, however, to read Law and Pascal.

Wednesday, July 4. I returned to London.

Sunday, July 8. Near ten thousand, by computation, gave diligent heed to the Word preached in Moorfields: 'Thou shalt call His name Jesus; for He shall save His people from their sins.' Numbers seemed greatly affected. Walking over an open field to Kennington Common, I was met by a man, who threatened me for a trespass. I preached 'Christ our wisdom, righteousness, sanctification, and redemption,' to double my morning congregation: and the Lord Almighty bowed their hearts before Him.

Monday, July 9. I corrected Mr. Cennick's hymns for the press.

Tuesday, July 10. I stopped Oakley, just going to Germany; and brought him quite off his design. Mrs. H., a brand plucked out of the burning through my brother's ministry, told me her wonderful history, which filled my heart with pity and love.

Saturday, July 14. Many were pierced through this evening with the sword of the Spirit, which is the Word of God.

Sunday, July 15. My subject in Moorfields was, God was in Christ, reconciling the world unto Himself; on the Common, Blessed are the poor in spirit.

Sunday, July 22. I never knew till now the strength of temptation, and energy of sin. Who, that conferred with flesh and blood, would covet great success? I live in a continual storm. My soul is always in my hand. The enemy thrusts sore at me, that I may fall; and a worse enemy than the devil is my own heart. *Miror aliquem praedicatorem salvari!* I received, I humbly hope, a fresh pardon in the sacrament at St. Paul's. I would have preached at the Fleet; but the Warden forbad. I preached at the Marshalsea.

Monday, July 23. I talked in Newgate with five condemned malefactors.

Wednesday, July 25. I was served with a writ by Mr. Goter, for walking over his field to Kennington. I sent Oakley to the lawyer, who confessed he did not so much as know what his client sued me for.

I saw Dr. Doddridge at Mr. Burnham's; but did not see much of him.

Thursday, July 26. The Lord applied His Word at Bray's, so that one received forgiveness under it.

Saturday, August 4. I dined with my friend George Whitefield at Mrs. Sparrow's, in Lewisham. In the evening at Mrs. Euster's; whom I visit most days for my own sake.

Sunday, August 5. In the fields, I discoursed on the promise, I will pray the Father, and He shall send you another Comforter. My subject was the same at Kennington. In the bands, one witnessed her having received her pardon. We gave thanks with her, whom the Lord hath redeemed.

Tuesday, August 7. I preached repentance and faith at Plaistow: and at night expounded, in a private house, Lazarus dead and raised. The next day I called with Hodges on Thomas Keen, a mild and candid Quaker: preached at Marybone. Too well pleased with my success, which brought upon me the buffetings of Satan. I preached on Kennington Common, Repent ye, and believe the gospel.

Friday, August 10. I gave George Whitefield some account both of my labours and my conflicts.

'Dear George, I forgot to mention the most material occurrence at Plaistow; namely, that a clergyman was there convinced of sin. He stood under me, and appeared, throughout my discourse, under the strongest perturbation of mind. In our return we were much delighted with an old spiritual Quaker, who is clear in justification by faith only. At Marybone a footman was convinced of more than sin; and now waits with confidence for all the power of faith. Friend Keen seems to have experience, and is right in the foundation.

'I cannot preach out on the week-days for the expense of coach, nor accept of dear Mr. Seward's offer; to which I should be less back ward, would he take my advice. But while he is so lavish of his Lord's goods, I cannot consent that this ruin should in any degree seem to be under my hand.

'I am continually tempted to leave off preaching, and hide myself like J. Hutchins. I should then be freer from temptation, and at leisure to attend my own improvement. God continues to work *by* me, but not *in* me, that I can perceive. Do not reckon upon me, my brother, in the work God is doing: for I cannot expect He should long employ one who is ever longing and murmuring to be discharged. I rejoice in your success, and pray for its increase a thousand fold.'

To-day I carried J. Bray to Mr. Law, who resolved all his feelings and experiences into fits or natural affections, and advised him to take no notice of his comforts, which he had better be without than with. He blamed Mr. Whitefield's Journals, and way of proceeding; said, he had had great hopes that the Methodists would have been dispersed by little and little into livings, and have leavened the whole lump. I told him my experience. 'Then am I,' said he, 'far below you (if you are right), not worthy to bear your shoes.' He agreed to our notion of faith, but would have it that all men held it: was fully against the laymen's expounding, as the very worst thing, both for themselves and others. I told him he was my schoolmaster to bring me to Christ; but the reason why I did not come sooner to Him was, my seeking to be sanctified before I was justified. I disclaimed all expectation of becoming some great one.

Among other things, he said, 'Was I so talked of as Mr. Whitefield is, I should run away, and hide myself entirely.' 'You might,' I answered; 'but God would bring you back like Jonah.' Joy in the Holy Ghost, he told us, was the most dangerous thing God could give. I replied, 'But cannot God guard His own gifts?' He often disclaimed advising, 'seeing we had the Spirit of God'; but mended upon our hands, and at last came almost quite over.

Sunday, August 12. I received power, great power, to explain the good Samaritan. I communicated at St. Paul's, as every Sunday. I convinced multitudes at the Common from 'Such were some of you; but ye are washed,' &c.; and before the day was past, felt my own sinfulness so great, that I wished I had never been born.

Monday, August 13. I wrote, in a letter to Seward, 'I preached yesterday to more than ten thousand hearers: am so buffeted, both before and after, that, was I not forcibly detained, I should fly from every human face. If God does make a way for me to escape, I shall not easily be brought back again. I cannot like advertising. It looks like sounding a trumpet.

'I hope our brother Hutchins will come forth at last, and throw away, which he seems to have taken up, my mantle of reserve. But then he will no longer make Mr. Broughton his counsellor.

Tuesday, August 14. I carried Cossart, a Moravian, to Mr. Law, and left them together. The whole congregation at Kennington seemed moved by my discourse on those words, 'He shall reprove the world of sin, of righteousness, and of judgement.' I could hardly get from them. We hear every day of more and more convinced or pardoned.

Wednesday, August 15. I wrote to George Whitefield, 'Let not Cossart's opinion of your letter to the Bishop weaken your hands. *Abundans cautela nocet.* It is the Moravian infirmity. To-morrow I set out for Bristol. I pray you all a good voyage, and that many poor souls may be added to the church by your ministry, before we meet again. Meet again, I am confident we shall;

perhaps both here and in America. The will of the Lord be done with us, and by us, in time and in eternity.'

I called on our brother Bell, just as his wife received 'like precious faith.' We were all partakers of her joy.

Thursday, August 16. I rode to Wycombe; and, being refused the church, would have preached in an house; but Bowers's preaching here has shut the door against me, by confirming their natural aversion to the gospel. The next day we came to Oxford, and the day after that to Evesham.

I sent my brother and friends accounts of our going on from time to time: the following to my brother:

'Bengeworth and Evesham, August 20, 1739.

'Dear Brother, We left the brethren at Oxford much edified, and two gownsmen, besides C. Graves, thoroughly awakened. On Saturday afternoon God brought us hither. Mr. Seward being from home, there was no admittance for us, his wife being an opposer, and having refused to see G. Whitefield before me. At seven Mr. Seward found us at our inn, and carried us home. I expounded at eight in the schoolroom, which contains two hundred; and held out the promises from John xvi.: "I will send the Comforter," &c.

'On Sunday morning I preached from George Whitefield's pulpit, the wall, "Repent ye, and believe the gospel." The notice being short, we had only a few hundreds, but such as those described in the morning lesson, "These were more noble than those of Thessalonica, in that they received the word with all readiness of mind." In the evening I showed to near two thousand their Saviour in the good Samaritan. Many, I am persuaded, found themselves stripped, and wounded, and half-dead: and are therefore ready for the oil and wine. Once more God strengthened me at nine to open the new covenant at the school-house, which was crowded with deeply attentive sinners.'

Monday, August 20. I spoke from Acts ii. 37 to two or three hundred market-people and soldiers; all as orderly and decent as could be desired. I now heard that the Mayor had come down on Sunday to take a view of us; and soon after an officer struck a countryman in the face, without any provocation. A serious woman besought the poor man not to resist evil, as the other only wanted to make a riot. He took patiently several repeated blows, telling the man he might beat him as long as he pleased.

I took a walk with Mr. Seward, whose eyes it has pleased God to open, to see He would have all men to be saved. His wife, who refuses to see me, is miserably bigoted to the particular scheme.

We had the satisfaction of meeting with Mr. Seward's cousin Molly, whom I had endeavoured to convince of sin at Islington. The Spirit has now convinced her of righteousness also. To-day she told us a young lady here upon a visit had been deeply struck on Sunday night, under the Word, seeing and feeling her need of a physician; and earnestly desired me to pray for her. We immediately joined in thanksgiving and intercession. After dinner I spoke with her. She burst into tears; told us she had come hither thoughtless and dead in pleasures and sin, but fully resolved against ever being a Methodist; that she was first alarmed at seeing us so happy and full of love; had gone to the Society, but never found herself out, till the Word came with power to her soul; that all the following night she had been as in an agony; could not pray; could not bear our singing, nor have any rest in her spirit. We betook ourselves to prayer; and God hearkened. She received forgiveness in that instant, and triumphed in the name of the Lord *her* God. We were all of us upon the mount the rest of the day.

At six I explained the nature of faith from 'Not I, but Christ liveth in me, Who loved *me,* and gave Himself for *me.*' Afterwards I showed them, in the school-house, their own case in dead Lazarus. Some of those that were dead, I trust, begin to come forth. Several serious people from the neighbouring towns came home with us. We continued our rejoicings till midnight.

Tuesday, August 21. I besought my hearers to be reconciled unto God. I found Miss P. had been greatly strengthened by last night's expounding, and could scarce forbear crying out, 'She was that Lazarus; and if they would come to Christ, He would raise them, as He had her.' All night she continued singing in her heart; and discovers more and more of that genuine mark of His disciples, love.

I was prevailed upon to stay over this day. God soon showed us *His* design in it. Our singing in the garden drew two sincere women to us, who sought Christ sorrowing. After reading the promises in Isaiah, we prayed, and they received them accomplished in themselves. We were upon a mount, which reminded us of Tabor, through the joy wherewith our Master filled us. How shall I be thankful enough for His bringing me hither! While we were singing, a poor drunken servant of Mr. Seward's was struck. His master had last night given him warning; but now he seems effectually called. We spent the afternoon most delightfully in Isaiah. At seven the Society met. I could hardly speak through my cold; but it was suspended, while I showed the natural man his picture in blind Bartimeus. Many were ready to cry after Jesus for mercy. The three that had lately received their sight were much strengthened. Miss P. declared her cure before two hundred witnesses; many of them gay young gentlewomen. They received her testimony, flocked round about her, and pressed her on all sides to come to see them. By this open confession, she purchased to herself great boldness in the faith.

Wednesday, August 22. This morning the work upon poor Robin appeared to be God's work. The words that made the first impression were:

'Tis mercy all, immense and free,
For, O my God, it found out me!

He now seems full of sorrow, and joy, and astonishment, and love. The world, too, set to their seal that he belongs to Christ.

Here I cannot but observe the narrow spirit of those that hold particular redemption. I have had no disputes with them, yet they have me in abomination. Mrs. Seward is irreconcilably angry with me; 'for he offers Christ to all.' Her maids are of the same spirit; and their Baptist teacher insists that I ought to have my gown stripped over my ears.

When Mr. Seward, in my hearing, exhorted one of the maids to a concern for her salvation, she answered, 'It was to no purpose; she could do nothing.' The same answer he received from his daughter, of seven years old. See the genuine fruits of this blessed doctrine!

Gloucester, August 23.

'By ten last night the Lord brought us hither through many dangers and difficulties. In mounting, I fell over my horse, and sprained my hand. Riding in the dark, I bruised my foot. We lost our way as often as we *could*. Two horses we had between three; for Robin bore us company. Here we were turned back from a friend's house by his wife's sickness. Last night my voice and strength wholly failed me. To-day they are in some measure restored. At night I with difficulty got into the crowded Society; preached the law and the gospel from Rom. iii. They received it with all readiness. Three clergymen were present. Some without attempted to make a disturbance by setting on the dogs, but in vain: the *dumb* dogs rebuked the rioters.'

Gloucester, August 25.

'Before I went forth into the streets and high ways, I sent, after my custom, to borrow the church. The minister (one of the better disposed) sent back a civil message, that he would be glad to drink a glass of wine with me, but durst not lend me his pulpit for fifty guineas.

'Mr. Whitefield durst lend me his field, which did just as well. For near an hour and a half God gave me voice and strength to exhort about two thousand sinners to repent and believe the gospel. My voice and strength failed together; neither do I want them when my work is done. Being invited to Painswick, I waited upon the Lord, and renewed my strength. We found near one thousand gathered in the street. I have but one subject, on which I discoursed from 2 Cor. v. 19: "God was in Christ, reconciling the world unto Himself." I besought them earnestly to be reconciled, and the rebels seemed inclinable to lay down their arms. A young Presbyterian teacher clave to us. I received fresh strength to expound the good Samaritan at a public-house, which was full above stairs and below.'

Saturday, August 25. I showed them in the street that to them and to their children was the promise made. Some are, I trust, on the point of receiving it. Three clergymen attended. I prayed by a young woman, afraid of death, because it had not lost its sting. I showed her the promise was to those that are afar off, even *before* they actually receive it; if they can but trust that they *shall* receive it. This revived her much; and we left her patiently waiting for the salvation of God.

At nine I exhorted and prayed with an house full of sincere souls; and took my leave, recommended by their affectionate prayers to the grace of God.

At Gloucester I received an invitation from F. Drummond. I dined with her and several of the friends, particularly Josiah Martin, a spiritual man, as far as I can discern. My heart was enlarged, and knit to them in love. I went to the field at five. An old intimate acquaintance (Mrs. Kirkham) stood in my way, and challenged me, What, Mr. Wesley, is it you I see? Is it possible that you who can preach at Christ Church, St. Mary's, &c., should come hither after a mob? I cut her short with, The work which my Master giveth me, must I not do it? and went to my mob, or (to put it in the Pharisees phrase) this people which is accursed. Thousands heard me gladly, while I told them their privilege of the Holy Ghost, the Comforter, and exhorted them to come for Him to Christ as poor lost sinners. I continued my discourse till night.

'Runwick, *August* 26.

'The minister here lent me his pulpit. I stood at the window (which was taken down), and turned to the larger congregation of above two thousand, in the churchyard. They appeared greedy to hear, while I testified, "God so loved the world, that He gave His only-begotten Son," &c. These are, I think, more noble than those at Evesham.

'After sermon, a woman came to me who had received faith in hearing Mr. Whitefield. She was terrified at having lost her comfort. I explained to her that wilderness-state into which the believer is *generally* led by the Spirit to be tempted, as soon as he is baptized by the Holy Ghost. This confirmed her in a patient looking for His return whom her soul loveth.

'We dined at Mr. Ellis's of Ebly. I met our brother Ellis, who has the blessing of believing parents; two sisters awakened; one only brother continues an abandoned prodigal. In the afternoon I preached again to a Kennington congregation. The church was full as it could crowd. Thousands stood in the churchyard. It was the most beautiful sight I ever beheld. The people filled the gradually rising area, which was shut up on three sides by a vast perpendicular hill. On the top and bottom of this hill was a circular row of trees. In this amphitheatre they stood, deeply attentive, while I called upon them in Christ's words, "Come unto Me, all that are weary." The tears of many testified that they were ready to enter into that rest. God enabled me to lift up my voice like a trumpet; so that all distinctly heard me. I concluded with singing an invitation to sinners.

'It was with difficulty we made our way through this most loving people, and returned amidst their prayers and blessings to Ebly. Here I expounded the second lesson for two hours, and received strength and faith to plead the promise of the Father. A good old Baptist pressed me to preach at Stanley, in my way to Bristol.' Accordingly,

Monday, August 27. I set out at seven. The sky was overcast, and the Prince of the power of the air wetted us to the skin. This, I thought, portended good. We could not stay to dry ourselves, there being, contrary to our expectation, a company of near one thousand waiting. I preached from a table (having been first denied the pulpit), upon, 'Repent, and believe the gospel.' The hearers seemed so much affected that I appointed them to meet me again in the evening. The minister was of my audience.

I rode back to Ebly, and was informed by brother Oakley that he had fastened upon the poor prodigal, and spoke to his heart. His convictions were heightened by the sermon. We prayed and sang alternately, till faith came. God blew with His wind, and the waters flowed. He struck the hard rock, and the waters gushed out, and the poor sinner, with joy and astonishment, believed the Son of God loved him, and gave Himself for him. Sing, ye heavens, for the Lord hath done it; shout, ye lower parts of the earth!

In the morning I had told his mother the story of St. Austin's conversion. Now I carried her the joyful news, 'This thy son was dead, and is alive again.' I expounded at a gentlewoman's house, in my way to Stanley, but could hardly speak through my cold. I went forth in faith, and preached under a large elm-tree, on the prodigal son, and returned to Ebly rejoicing; where I expounded the woman of Samaria.

www.ingramcontent.com/pod-product-compliance
Lightning Source LLC
Chambersburg PA
CBHW051835040426
42447CB00006B/541